The Unique Christ

Volume Two

volume two

THE UNIQUE CHRIST

Nizar Shaheen

CASTLE QUAY BOOKS
CANADA

crossroads
FAMILY OF MINISTRIES

THE UNIQUE CHRIST – *Volume Two*

Printed in Canada
International Standard Book Number: 1-894860-12-8

Castle Quay Books
1740 Pilgrim's Way, Oakville, Ontario, L6M 1S5
Tel: (416) 573-3249 Fax: (519) 748-9835
E-mail: info@castlequaybooks.com
www.castlequaybooks.com
and
Crossroads Christian Communications, Inc.
P.O. Box 5100, Burlington, Ontario, Canada, L7R 4M2
Tel: (905) 332-6400
E-mail: huntley@crossroads.ca
www.crossroads.ca

Cover design by John Cowie, *eyetoeye, design;* and Andrew Morrow, *Visualeyes Communications.*
Copy editing by Janet Dimond and Karen Stowell.

National Library of Canada Cataloguing in Publication

Shaheen, Nizar
The Unique Christ: Volume 2 / Nizar Shaheen.
Co-published by Crossroads Christian Communications, Inc.
Includes bibliographical references.
ISBN 1-894860-12-8 (v. 2)

1. Jesus Christ – Person and offices – Biblical teaching.
I. Dimond, Janet II. Crossroads Christian Communications III. Title.

BT203.S43 2003 232 C2003-900461-9

Dedication

To my wife, Ellen, who is my partner in this project and who spent countless hours typing. I thank her for her love, support, and commitment.

Thanks

To my wonderful children for their patience and understanding.

Glory and Praise

To my Lord Jesus Christ for His blessings, goodness, and immeasurable love.

Table of Contents

Foreword

September 11th, 2001 changed the world. Media personalities often gave uninformed statements about the religion of Islam. Muslim leaders showed up on every talk show in a damage control effort.

Meanwhile, on *100 Huntley Street*, a daily and nightly TV hour, I invited the Middle-Eastern Bible scholar, Nizar Shaheen, to comment. It was four months before 9/11 that I met King Abdullah of Jordan. When he learned of my connection with Nizar Shaheen, this king of a Muslim country said these words: "Nizar is a great man of God. I watch him all the time on television."

Since the attack on the World Trade Center, I've been asked over and over, "What do Muslims believe?" I'm not an expert on the Islamic religion, but I do know Mohammed taught that Jesus was not God's Son. He said that Jesus was a prophet like himself, believing that God has no Son. Mohammed also taught that Jesus didn't die on the cross. And of course, that meant no resurrection and no substitutionary sacrifice for the forgiveness of our sins.

As I prayed about our public response, it became clear to me that the best answer was to present the facts about Jesus without reference to the beliefs of Mohammed – beliefs which originated over 600 years after Jesus ascended to the right hand of the Father where He now prays for us.

Therefore, the obvious choice for such a series was Nizar Shaheen. Nizar was born in Nazareth, the home of Jesus as a youth. He was raised in Cana of Galilee, the place of Jesus' first miracle. While Nizar was a university student in Haifa, he faced death at least three times – once in a fall from a high point of a mosque, and twice from car accidents. Each time as his life was spared, he heard a voice saying in the Arabic language, *"Fear not, for I have redeemed you. I have called you by your name; you are Mine."* When it was pointed out to him that these were the words found in the Bible, Isaiah 43:1, he made a full commitment to Jesus as his Saviour and Lord.

Nizar, a boxing champion of the Galilee region, was in the habit of running 15 km in the early morning. Unable to continue boxing because of injuries, he turned his attention to studying the Bible, reading it cover to cover once a month for an entire year. Upon completing this Bible reading "marathon" for the twelfth time, he heard the voice of the Lord again...this time calling him into the ministry of Jesus Christ.

When I first met Nizar at the Jerusalem University College, he was well on his way. He studied in Cyprus and in Europe and was ordained to the ministry at the Nazareth Baptist Church. He has produced and hosted an Arabic language TV ministry for 14 years, covering most of the

Arabic-speaking world. He has taught through the Bible in English, chapter by chapter, on *100 Huntley Street* over a four-year period, 1990 to 1994.

Through 2002, Nizar has presented *The Unique Christ*, a series of teachings from Scripture with powerful and irrefutable logic, across Canada and the U.S.A. on several TV networks. Television is good, but to read, mark and meditate on a book is also important for the intelligent, inquiring mind.

Nizar is a man truly called of God, whose destiny is to change the thinking of millions of precious people. My prayer is that God's Spirit of truth will take the compelling words of this book and illuminate them to both your mind and heart.

DAVID MAINSE
Host of *100 Huntley Street*

Introduction

JESUS CHRIST was truly unique. In fact, He is the greatest historical figure of all time. How amazing that it was a carpenter who had the greatest influence on humankind and history. But Jesus was much more than just a carpenter, *"for in Him dwells all the fullness of the Godhead bodily"* (Colossians 2:9).

Jesus is the sinless God-Man; everything about Him is unique. To fully speak of Him would take all eternity. At the conclusion of John's Gospel account, he said,

> *...there are also many other things that Jesus did, which if they were written one by one, I suppose that even the world itself could not contain the books that would be written* (John 21:25).

In words of prophecy concerning the Messiah Jesus, the psalmist sang: *"You are fairer than the sons of men; grace is poured upon Your lips; therefore God has blessed You for-*

ever.... I will make Your name to be remembered in all generations; therefore the people shall praise You forever and ever (Psalm 45:17).

The goal of this book, *The Unique Christ, Volume Two*, is to continue to uplift, praise, and glorify the Lord Jesus. The truth and beauty of His teachings are unsurpassed. He is a fascinating Person to study. His words bring life and light (John 1:4; 8:12). It is insightful and rewarding to delve into a study of His uniqueness. I only ask that, before you read the teachings, you pause and pray that God would open your mind, heart and spirit, and give you greater faith and understanding of spiritual things. *"And the apostles said to the Lord, 'Increase our faith'"* (Luke 17:5). How much more we need to ask the same of the Lord Jesus. May God bless you.

NIZAR SHAHEEN
Host of *Light For All Nations*

Chapter 1

Jesus Christ and True Freedom

EVERYONE shouts for freedom – freedom of expression, freedom from military occupation, freedom of choice, freedom of religion. When it is a matter of truth and justice, then the shouts for freedom are justified. Many times, however, the freedom people are seeking is not freedom at all. There are those who shout for freedom of choice, such as the choice to abort an unwanted unborn child, or to use illegal drugs. Sometimes what they think is freedom is actually enslavement or taking away the freedom of another, and that is not justice. Jesus said, *"Whoever commits sin is a slave of sin"* (John 8:34). So, if sin enslaves, then righteousness sets us free.

How does humankind become righteous? The Bible teaches that it is impossible for man to be righteous apart from God, and we can only become righteous through Jesus Christ (Romans 3:22). This is exactly what Jesus taught. He said,

> *If you abide in My word, you are My disciples indeed. And you shall know the truth, and the truth shall make you free* (John 8:31,32).

Apart from truth, there is no real and true freedom. Jesus also said that He is the Truth (John 14:6; 1:17). So to be truly free, we must be disciples of Jesus and abide in Him (John 15:7), meaning we are to learn everything that Jesus teaches, and to internalize and live by it.

In the same teaching recorded by John, Jesus continued to tell the people, *"Therefore if the Son makes you free, you shall be free indeed"* (John 8:36). That word "*indeed*" serves as an exclamation mark. It is something new and exciting that Jesus was teaching the people. They were enslaved to sin, to vain tradition and meaningless religious practices, to self-righteousness, and to the social injustice of that day.

The Pharisees, who were the religious leaders, were full of pride and self-righteousness as descendants from Abraham. They would not admit that they needed to be delivered from anything, nor did they agree that they needed Jesus to give them freedom (John 8:33). Jesus spoke the truth and showed that they were not true children of Abraham, nor were they children of God, for they were slaves to sin. To be a child of God, one must accept Jesus and believe in His name. It makes no difference if you claim to be descended from Abraham; what matters is our spiritual descent (John 1:12).

Like the Pharisees in Jesus' day, many people today will not admit that they need deliverance. They are complacent and think they are free to do as they please and live in disobedience to God. This is the way to destruction and enslavement. By following Jesus' teachings, all the things that cause enslavement are abolished.

Concerning social injustice, Jesus had righteous anger when He cleared the temple courts of wickedness and condemned the dishonest merchants and money-changers who were abusing the people (Matthew 21:12,13). Jesus also condemned strongly the religious hypocrites. But in Scripture we learn,

> *There is therefore now no condemnation to those who are in Christ Jesus, who do not walk according to the flesh, but according to the Spirit. For the law of the Spirit of life in Christ Jesus has* ***made me free*** *from the law of sin and death* (Romans 8:1,2).

In both cases, there is law – the law of Christ, which leads to freedom and life, and the law of sin which leads to bondage and death.

God created humankind to follow laws and to serve somebody. He also created everyone to have the freedom to choose Him and follow His Son, or to reject Him. It is of eternal significance for us to accept the love of God through His Son Jesus, and to serve God and be a slave to righteousness – for this leads to life! We learn in the divinely inspired teaching of the Apostle Paul:

> *Do you not know that to whom you present yourselves slaves to obey, you are that one's slaves whom you obey, whether of sin to death, or of obedience to righteousness? ...And* ***having been set free from sin, you became slaves of righteousness****...and the end, everlasting life* (Romans 6:16,18,22b; 2 Peter 2:19).

Our true freedom comes when we become servants or slaves of righteousness, which only comes by following the Lord Jesus and making Him Lord of our lives.

At the beginning of His ministry, Jesus explained what He had come to do, saying:

> *The Spirit of the Lord is upon Me...He has sent Me...to preach deliverance to the captives and recovery of sight to the blind, to set at liberty those who are oppressed* (Luke 4:18).

Jesus brought a message of freedom – inner freedom – freedom from the yoke of sin and corruption. At the time Jesus spoke His wonderful words of truth and life, much of the world was enslaved by the Roman Empire. Many people who became believers in Jesus were slaves, yet they still had true inner freedom.

When Jesus began His public ministry and gained popularity by performing miracles, many people followed Him in hopes that He would bring them political freedom from Roman oppression; but this was not Jesus' intention. The freedom He offered was a greater and more fulfilling freedom.

From what does Jesus free us?

1. **The bondage of sin.** When Jesus defeated Satan by His atoning work on the cross, we were set free from the power and guilt of sin. We are given a new life that "*sin might be done away with, that we should no longer be slaves of sin*" (Romans 6:6).

2. **Fear** (Romans 8:15). Fear of the unknown and fear of death (Hebrews 2:15), for because of Jesus, we have the assurance of eternal life with Him.

3. **Old Testament Law** and its burden, requirements and curse (Romans 6:14; 7:6; Galatians 3:10; 5:18). No per-

son, except Jesus, could completely keep the Law which revealed our sin and made us guilty. But Jesus fulfilled the Law and imputed His righteousness to us, so believers in Jesus do not stand condemned by the Law.

4. **The realm of Satan** and the power of darkness, that we might enter *"into the kingdom of the Son of His love"* (Colossians 1:13).

5. **The curse** that is upon the earth because of sin (Romans 8:21). At His Second Coming, Jesus will bring freedom to all creation.

Jesus was a gift from God sent to the earth, and freedom is also a gift of God which comes from knowing the truth. Jesus is the truth. In the beginning of the Christian church, the powerful Gospel message of God's love and truth spread rapidly and conquered the hearts of millions. God did not want His message to be spread through fear, the power of the sword, or by violence, as some religions have done in the past. This does not cause a true change in anyone's heart. The change comes when we believe in Jesus, obey God's Word in the Bible, and grow in spiritual knowledge, which then leads us to grow in freedom from sin.

The cross of Jesus Christ is the solution for man to be set free. As believers in Jesus, we are crucified with Christ and die to self, fleshly desires, and the sins of the world (Galatians 2:20; 5:24; 6:14). Maybe you have not received the freedom that Jesus gives? Call upon Him, for He has the power to deliver you from anything that holds you enslaved: a bad habit, violent temper, selfish desires, lust, superstitions, or even your traditions or customs. What is unique about Jesus Christ is that He is the Greatest Liberator! When you believe in Him and put your faith in

Him, He will not only deliver you from the bondage of sin, but will give you His righteousness – the righteousness of God – that you might live in true freedom. For *"if the Son makes you free, you shall be free indeed!"* (John 8:36).

Chapter 2

JESUS CHRIST AND TRUE PEACE

FROM THE moment Adam sinned and a sinful nature was imputed to humankind, the world has lacked peace. People throughout all the ages have been putting forth unsuccessful efforts to find that peace. In the Bible, God has said, *"There is no peace...for the wicked"* (Isaiah 57:21). The Apostle James writes:

> *Where do wars and fights come from among you? Do they not come from your desires for pleasure that war in your members* [or from within yourself]? (James 4:1).

The Scripture continues to point out that the root factor for lack of peace is sin, and specifically mentioned are wrongful pride, lust, and greed.

Since the Second World War, the world has been trying to end all wars, yet there have been about 45 wars waged. This is far more than ever before within such a short period of time in history. Many thought that with the industrial revolution, the new prosperity, and the advancement of knowledge, the world would finally experience peace; but the opposite happened. In fact, the highest percentage of suicides today are in the most advanced and supposedly "peaceful" countries of the world. People clearly do not have peace.

Peace Defined

So what is peace? Let us first consider what peace is not. It is not running from difficulties or the avoidance of pain or persecution, or hiding in a safe place. Peace is not only the absence of war and trials, but means wholeness or completeness. It includes rest, health, safety, and prosperity. True peace is the peace of God which comes from Jesus, the Prince of Peace (Isaiah 9:7), as the Old Testament prophesied. When you enjoy the peace of God, it is a peace which passes all natural understanding. It is exceedingly great joy; it is sufficiency and contentment, regardless of your situation.

When Jesus was in the Upper Room just hours before His arrest, He foreknew all the terrible things that would happen to Him. Yet He still had peace. However, He sensed that His disciples were sad and distressed. Even though He had promised them the coming of the Comforter (the Holy Spirit), mansions in heaven, and the fact that He would return to take them with Him, for the present time they still needed something else. So Jesus promised them another gift, and it was the necessary and precious gift of peace. He said, *"Peace I leave with you, My peace I give to you; not as the world gives do I give to you"* (John 14:27a).

There is a big difference between the peace that the world gives and the peace that Jesus gives. What is the peace that the world has to offer? It is a temporal, unsatisfying form of peace that is ineffective and powerless. It is based on economic resources and diplomatic relationships, such as cease-fire agreements or trade relationships. It is based on how the individuals or countries involved benefit, such as with strength, materialism, and prosperity. Often this type of peace is really just the strong crushing the weak because of greed. This peace usually does not last long, and it is often counterfeit.

One of the main differences between worldly peace and Jesus' peace is that the world enjoys peace through the absence of troubles, positive thinking, or a good feeling. But the believer enjoys peace despite the troubles that surround him. We don't need to play mind games to have a sense of peace, since we are filled with the presence of God and the power of the Holy Spirit. God's peace is a confident assurance that in any situation, present or future, we need not fear, for God is with us. He gives us the grace and the peace to endure any difficulty, and to even rejoice in tribulation, which is like sharing in the suffering of Jesus, or taking up our cross. For the believer, there is peace in the midst of the storm, like Jesus who was sleeping in the boat while the terrible storm surrounded Him (Mark 4:35-41).

God created the world with such great resources, and gave abilities to humankind to benefit and tend to His creation. If the godly way was followed, and if there was no greed, then there would not be one starving person in the world – no one would ever lack for anything. Even the United Nations, with all its efforts, has not been able to bring peace or ease the suffering in the world. Jesus said, *"My peace,"* for the world has no peace, and yet it tries to offer something it does not possess. How can someone give something they lack? How can the blind lead the blind?

How does one attain peace?

- from the work that Jesus accomplished on the cross
- from the indwelling of the Holy Spirit
- it is a promise of God in Scripture
- it is a gift from God through Jesus
- it is an inheritance that Jesus, the Good Shepherd, left to His disciples
- it is a blessing.

Who can receive this divinely bestowed peace? In the Bible we learn that it is those who are believers in Jesus whose sins have been forgiven by the Lord. Having been reconciled to God through the atoning work of Jesus that He accomplished on the cross, every person who seeks Him with a repentant heart is entitled to it. Like salvation, peace is a gift from God. In Scripture, we read: *"Therefore, having been justified by faith, we have peace with God through our Lord Jesus Christ"* (Romans 5:1). When we accept Jesus as our Saviour, we enjoy the gift of peace which includes:

- peace with God
- peace with others
- peace within
- peace with all creation.

Peace with God is what so many religions of the world try to offer. In the Holy Bible, we learn that humankind, apart from Jesus Christ, is far from God and without hope.

> *But now in Christ Jesus you who once were far off have been made near by the blood of Christ. For He Himself is our peace...*(Ephesians 2:13,14).

Ironically, King David's reign was one of much war and yet he said, *"Seek peace, and pursue it"* (Psalm 34:14). I believe He was speaking of spiritual peace. He spoke prophetically about seeking after God through Jesus Christ, and not just to look for God's peace, but to actively pursue it.

Immediately after Jesus promised to give His disciples peace, He said, *"Let not your heart be troubled, neither let it be afraid"* (John 14:27b). This divinely bestowed peace does not co-exist with fear and troubles. The peace of Jesus is stronger than all the circumstances that come from the outside, such as poverty, sickness, or persecution. In fact, the disciples to whom Jesus spoke directly were all going to face persecution and even death. However, the peace Jesus had given them was lasting, even to the very end of their lives and beyond into eternity.

The peace of Jesus is also stronger than anything that comes from within, like a guilty conscience, or accusations of the enemy. It is an all-encompassing peace within one's heart, soul, and mind. What a wonderful peace you experience when you know that your sins are forgiven! What a restful place it is to be when you trust in God and in His leading for your life, having the Holy Spirit to guide you, and thus allowing God to have full control. What a great peace it is to know your destiny. The believer in Jesus has been promised by God that he or she will inherit eternal life. Therefore, one need not fear death. Also, what a great peace it is to the soul, to know that through the Lord Jesus, there is victory over sin and a victorious life as a citizen in God's kingdom. This peace makes the believer unshakable and provides confidence and calmness in one's heart. When this peace of God is within, it serves as a guard to keep both the heart and mind holy. We read in Scripture, *"The peace of*

God, which surpasses all understanding, will guard your hearts and minds through Christ Jesus" (Philippians 4:7).

The Example of Jesus

Jesus' life was characterized by peace. He had a balanced and pure life. He was calm, patient, and had self-control. He was the embodiment of peace. He fulfilled and brought the blessing of peace which God spoke of in the Old Testament: *"The Lord bless you and keep you.... The Lord lift up His countenance upon you, and give you peace"* (Numbers 6:24,26).

The secret of Jesus' peace was His full obedience to the will of the Father. Jesus' message, the Good News, is a message of peace. After Jesus ascended into heaven, the message of the disciples became a message of peace. In fact, it is commonly called "The Gospel of Peace." One day, in His final victory, Jesus will destroy Satan (Romans 16:20), who is the source of troubles and warring, and He will establish His kingdom of peace, justice, and righteousness (Isaiah 9:6,7). The new Jerusalem will then truly be a city of peace, which is what the name Jerusalem means. In prophecy, we read:

> *They shall beat their swords into plowshares, and their spears into pruning hooks; nation shall not lift up sword against nation, neither shall they learn war anymore* (Isaiah 2:4).

Micah also prophesied of the ideal life of peace and comfort when Jesus reigns:

> *Everyone shall sit under his vine and under his fig tree, and no one shall make them afraid.... But we will walk in the name of the Lord our God forever and ever* (Micah 4:4,5).

Now, that's the life!

Through Jesus Christ, believers have a new nature; therefore, let us actively *"put on the new man,"* as Scripture exhorts (Colossians 3:10). One way in which we do this is through unity and with a conscious effort: *"And let the peace of God rule in your hearts, to which also you were called in one body; and be thankful"* (Colossians 3:15).

Jesus is the Christian's perfect example (1 Peter 2:21-23). He is the source of peace and the foundation of the believer's peace. Since Jesus is the source and He possesses peace, therefore, only He can give it. Are you a believer? Do you have this inner peace? Do you feel the tugging at your heart and know deep inside that you need Jesus as your Saviour? Then pray to Him with faith, believing in your heart that God has raised Him from the dead, and you shall be saved and experience His peace.

The peace of God is so important that from the beginning of the church, the word *peace* became the Christian blessing. It was always used in greetings, farewells, and in benedictions. You can read of this numerous times in the New Testament (Galatians 6:14-16; Ephesians 6:23; 1 Thessalonians 5:23; Romans 15:13,33; Hebrews 13:20,21). This is something we as Christians should continue today. *"Now may the Lord of peace Himself give you peace always in every way. The Lord be with you all"* (2 Thessalonians 3:16).

Chapter 3

Jesus Christ and True Worship

It is within the nature of humankind to be a worshipper. God created us that way, and intended for us to worship Him alone, for only God Almighty is worthy of worship (Psalm 29:2; Revelation 4:11). Adam was taught by God and knew how to worship Him. Abel, Abraham, and many others before Moses built altars to offer sacrifices in their worship. Then with Moses, God revealed a more complete way to worship Him. When the people were obedient to Him, He was pleased and satisfied with their worship. This was manifested by His presence in the Ark of the Covenant, the tabernacle in the wilderness, and in the temple in Jerusalem, when the cloud of His glory descended. But ever since sin entered the world, other things have replaced the true worship of God (Romans 1:25). Yet from the beginning, most of humankind has strived to come closer to God, for we have been created to glorify and praise Him (Isaiah 43:7,21; Psalm 29:1,2; 95:6; 96:7,8; 147:1; 148:13).

With the coming of Jesus into the world, a new revelation and a new age were ushered in. Through Him, we now behold the glory of God (John 1:14). In His marvellous teachings, He shed a new light on worship and gave it new meaning. Speaking to the Samaritan woman, He said,

> *The hour is coming, and now is, when the true worshippers will worship the Father in spirit and truth; for the Father is seeking such to worship Him* (John 4:23).

What does the Bible teach about worship?

1. **Where we worship.** It is not the location that is important. The centre of worship for the Samaritans was on Mount Gerazim and for the Jews it was on Mount Moriah, an extension of Mount Zion in Jerusalem. Jesus told the woman that "God is Spirit" (John 4:24), so He is not a physical being who is limited to space and time. He is present everywhere and can be worshipped anywhere at any time. To do so, does not require facing Jerusalem or any other direction.

2. **How we worship.**

   a. ***In truth.*** As Jesus taught, true worship has to be *"in truth."* It has to be real, genuine worship from the heart. Not hypocritical nor done for show, nor just going through the motions of prayer, which is meaningless. It is very important to realize that to worship in truth is to worship God through Jesus Christ. Jesus is the *Truth* of God (John 3:21; 14:6) and the only *Way* to God, the Father (Acts 4:12). You must know Jesus to worship in truth.

b. ***In spirit.*** We have been made in the spiritual image of God and, through the work of God's Holy Spirit in our lives, we can worship God *"in spirit,"* which is the kind of worship He desires. Worship in the spirit is not carnal. Also, when we are filled with the Holy Spirit, He empowers our worship and helps us to know how to pray (Romans 8:26; John 14:26). Since Jesus is present with us today, and since He sent the Holy Spirit to the believers, He has inaugurated and revealed a new realm of worship which is pleasing to God. In this new realm, we can have a deep fellowship with God through Jesus Christ and enjoy His blessings and His presence.

3. **Why we worship.**

a. ***Because of who God is*** – His person, His nature, and His attributes.

b. ***Because God commanded it, desires it, and deserves it.*** As Jesus said, *"the Father is seeking such [that is, true worshippers] to worship Him"* (John 4:23).

c. ***Because God created us.*** As we are made in His image, it is only right that we offer ourselves to Him in worship.

d. ***Because God provided for our salvation.*** We have been redeemed by Jesus and given eternal life in heaven. Express your thankfulness to God for your salvation when you worship Him.

e. ***Because God loves us.*** He is our Heavenly Father who takes a personal interest in us, and also cares for us, guides us, and has made Himself near to us. The fact that God is our Father is a new revelation that Jesus gave us.

f. ***Because we love God.*** This is expressed by obedience to Him, being in service for Him, praising Him with words and songs, and offering gifts to the Lord's work, which is a form of worship.

Since Jesus taught us about true worship, this implies that there must also be false worship. When Jesus spoke with the Samaritan woman, He was direct and firm in saying, "*You worship what you do not know*" (John 4:22).

The Samaritan's religion was confused and in error:

- It was a decapitated religion, since they were missing two-thirds of the holy-inspired Old Testament writings. They only believed in the five books of Moses, so they did not have the full revelation of God. They believed there was one true God and believed in His attributes. However, they rejected His promises and prophecies, so they could not fully know God.

- Their worship was based on ignorance. It was a futile, vain worship that became false and counterfeit. They chose what they wanted to believe and rejected what they could not understand.

- Their worship was built on superstitions, imaginations, unfounded fears, and vain traditions. It was not based on truth, knowledge or love for God. Therefore, their worship was not acceptable to Him.

When Jesus spoke with the Samaritan woman, He did not have the attitude that many Jews of His day had: "We're right and you're wrong." For Jesus knew that among His own people, the way in which they worshipped was also unacceptable to God. Jesus had to purify and cleanse the temple because of all the corruption. He had many strong words with the Jewish religious leaders of His day, and rebuked them because:

- They thought they were superior.
- They mistreated the Samaritans.
- They focussed on the *letter* of the Law rather than the *spirit* of the Law.
- They put a heavy burden on the people because of vain traditions.
- They were often hypocritical in the way they prayed in public so as to be seen by many, and proud in the pious way they dressed and fasted.
- Their worship became the socially acceptable thing and was done, not out of love for God, but out of fear – fear for their reputation, and possibly, even out of an unhealthy fear of God. The Bible teaches that we are to fear God, but this does not mean to be afraid of His wrath or punishment. It means to love, honour, and respect Him.

All people should learn from Jesus. The woman of Samaria certainly listened to Him, and understood what He was saying. It changed her life. Jesus broke down the barriers between the Jew and the Samaritan, and between the Jew and Gentile, for through Him everyone has the equal right to approach God. In Him, we are all one and can worship the Lord together in the same way.

In true worship to God, the Lord Jesus Christ is central. We have a promise from Jesus that when believers gather in His name to worship, He is *"there in the midst of them"*

(Matthew 18:20). Our worship then becomes a time of joy, celebration, praise, and thanksgiving to God. It is our natural response to God for all the wonderful things He has done, and for His many blessings. True worship is like offering up pleasing aromatic sacrifices to God. In the New Testament, it is called *"the sacrifice of praise"* (Hebrews 13:15). God no longer demands animal sacrifices and other offerings upon an altar. Jesus was the final and complete sacrifice for sins, and true worship is the sacrifice He now requires from His people. In true worship, we forget ourselves and focus on God. It is not merely something we do once a week when we gather together. It is a whole lifestyle and an attitude that exudes every area of our lives. Our worship of God should be something continuously in our thoughts and on our lips.

> *And whatever you do in word or deed, do all in the name of the Lord Jesus, giving thanks to God the Father through Him* (Colossians 3:17).

For the true worshipper, worship of God will never end. It will be continued in heaven, for God is forever worthy of praise (Revelation 7:11,12).

> *Therefore by Him [Jesus], let us continually offer the sacrifice of praise to God, that is, the fruit of our lips, giving thanks to His name* (Hebrews 13:15).

Chapter 4

Jesus and the Law

OUR LORD Jesus Christ was the greatest teacher of God's Law; even greater than Moses to whom the Law was originally given by direct revelation from God. The Law, called the Torah, consists of the first five books of the Jewish Scripture, the writings of Moses. These writings elaborate upon the fundamental laws that God gave Moses on Mount Sinai, namely, the Ten Commandments.

Why did God give the Law?

1. **To reveal His standards for holy and righteous living.**

2. **To preserve the people of God** and distinguish them as unique, special, and separated from others (Galatians 3:23,24).

3. **To reveal sin** and man's inadequacy to be righteous through his own personal achievements or works (Romans 3:19,20). The Law also reveals the ugliness

and severity of sin (Romans 7:7,13).

4. **To express His love** for His people (Exodus 19:5,6). The laws were given for their benefit.

5. **To reveal the way to worship Him** and how to be in right relationship with Him.

6. **To direct His people in their relationships with other people.**

7. **To reveal the value and equality of all human life**, including the protection of the defenceless, such as the widow, orphan, and stranger.

8. **To point people to their Saviour**, the Messiah, through whom they receive salvation, eternal life, and righteousness. Jesus said that Moses wrote about Him (John 5:39,46; Deuteronomy 18:18,19). Therefore, the Law clearly proves that man cannot save himself; he needs a Saviour.

The Law of God sets forth fundamental, moral principles for all humankind. Principles that are necessary, eternal, and universal; principles that are consistent with the very nature of God Himself. God is our Creator, and He knows humankind implicitly. He knows that we must have laws to govern our lives, or else we would live in a state of chaos and sin. God's laws comprise a complete, comprehensive and perfect system (Psalm 19:7-11). No one is to add to it, or take away from it (Deuteronomy 4:2). To break one command is to break them all and be cursed (James 2:10; Galatians 3:10; Deuteronomy 27:26). God's people are to preserve, study, honour, and obey His laws, and to be thankful to Him for giving them (Deuteronomy 4:2; 6:4-7;

8:6,10,11; 10:12-16; 11:1,13-23). God's Law is a delight; it is spiritual, holy, just, and good (Romans 7:12,14,22; Psalm 1:2).

Jesus honoured, obeyed, and taught the Law. He helped people to love the Law as well, and interpret it correctly. Unlike the religious leaders of His day, who taught the *letter of the Law* and its strict *outward* observance, Jesus concentrated on the *spirit of the Law* and its *inward* application. He taught that the whole Law was to love God and love your neighbour as yourself, and to follow the "Golden Rule" of doing unto others what you would have them do to you (Matthew 7:12).

At the beginning of His wonderful Sermon on the Mount, Jesus expressed His relationship to the Law:

> *Do not think that I came to destroy the Law or the Prophets. I did not come to destroy but to fulfill. For assuredly, I say to you, till heaven and earth pass away, one jot or one tittle will by no means pass from the law till all is fulfilled* (Matthew 5:17,18).

Jesus may have spoken these words directly to the Pharisees and scribes in the crowd who had accused Him of many things and tried to discredit Him before the people. Jesus clearly expressed that He did not annul the Law, and proved that while there was still a heaven and earth, every word of the Law is important. When He referred to the "*jot*" (the smallest Hebrew letter) and the "*tittle*" (a stroke of the pen that completes a letter and thus gives the word its correct meaning), He was showing that the words of the Law would remain forever, and are not to be changed. By saying this, Jesus must have silenced the Pharisees, at least for a short period of time.

The Pharisees were meticulous in their attempts to keep the Law, and by all outward appearances, they were the most holy of all men. They often accused Jesus and His disciples of breaking the Law, such as when Jesus healed on the Sabbath, visited in the homes of sinners, or when His disciples picked and ate grain on the Sabbath. Jesus, however, rebuked them for self-righteousness, hypocrisy, putting a heavy burden on the people, and breaking the Law of God because of all their vain traditions.

Yet Jesus Himself kept the Law, since He was born a Jew under the Law. In Scripture, we read: "*But when the fullness of the time had come, God sent forth His Son, born of a woman, born under the law, to redeem those who were under the law, that we might receive the adoption as sons*" (Galatians 4:4,5). Jesus proclaimed that He fulfilled the Law. In fact, He was the only person who could ever possibly keep the Law, since He was sinless (1 Peter 2:22-24; 2 Corinthians 5:21).

How did Jesus fulfill the Law?

1. **He kept the Law to perfection and performed everything prescribed by the Law.** When Jesus healed the man with leprosy, He instructed him to do as the Law commanded and show himself to a priest (Matthew 8:2-4). With the woman caught in adultery, the Pharisees set it up as a trap for Jesus, to catch Him breaking the Law (John 8). Curiously, the man involved in the adultery was not being accused; so by bringing just the woman before Jesus, they were not keeping the Law. The Law said that both persons involved were to be stoned and the accuser was to throw the first stone (Leviticus 20:10; Deuteronomy 22:22; 17:7). Jesus showed great wisdom,

for instead of judging the woman, He judged the accusers. How could such hypocrites judge and condemn the woman without judging themselves? Jesus wrote something in the dirt on the ground and, whatever it was, it convicted the men, pricked their consciences, and caused them to leave. Jesus forgave the woman and told her to sin no more. Yet He was not easy on sin and forgiveness did not come cheaply. Soon He was to die in her place – and in ours – so there would be full redemption.

2. **He gave the Law its full meaning and true significance.** This comes from within the heart with pure motivations; not merely an external observance without any change in the inner person.

3. **The Law pointed to Him.** Jesus fulfilled what the Law had spoken of concerning the Saviour (Romans 3:21,22; 10:4; Colossians 2:16,17).

4. **Through His vicarious death,** His substitutionary death upon the cross. The Old Testament Law required animal sacrifices, but the blood of animals was insufficient (Hebrews 10:4,11,12). All the sacrifices pointed to Jesus Christ, the Lamb who takes away the sin of the world (John 1:29). Jesus was the perfect, final, and complete sacrifice that fulfilled the demand and justice of God (see Hebrews 9:12-14; 10:1-4,12).

Jesus said to the people:

For I say to you, that unless your righteousness exceeds the righteousness of the scribes and Pharisees, you will by no means enter the kingdom of heaven (Matthew 5:20).

These words must have shocked the people who considered the Pharisees to be the most righteous and holy men. If their righteousness was not enough, was there hope for anyone else? They wrongly thought the Pharisees were better than others, when in actuality, because of the Law, everyone in the whole world was in the same situation – all are sinners and proven guilty (Romans 3:23). The fact is, humankind needs a Saviour! Jesus Christ came to be our Saviour and Redeemer! We read in the book of Galatians:

> *For as many as are of the works of the Law are under the curse; for it is written, "Cursed is everyone who does not continue in all things which are written in the book of the Law, to do them"* [Deuteronomy 27:26]. *But that no one is justified by the Law in the sight of God is evident, for "the just shall live by faith"* [Habakkuk 2:4].... *Christ has redeemed us from the curse of the Law, having become a curse for us* (Galatians 3:10,11,13).

On the cross, Jesus took all the sins of the world upon Himself and paid our penalty which the Law demanded for sin. He was victorious over sin in His resurrection from the dead. When we put our faith in Jesus, believe in Him, make Him Lord over our lives, and ask Him to forgive us our sins, He will. He also gives us strength to live a life that is pleasing to God through His Spirit. When we fall short, He is ready and willing to forgive us when we ask Him with a pure and sincere heart. This is *grace!* It is the *undeserved favour* of God because of the work Jesus did on the cross. *"For the law was given through Moses, but grace and truth came through Jesus Christ"* (John 1:17).

This is not to say that there was no grace in the Old Testament, for certainly there was. God's grace was evident in every animal sacrifice, and His truth came through the Law as well. But when Jesus came, truth and grace reached their fullness, and this same fullness is available to you. We are saved by grace, not the Law (Ephesians 2:8,9). Humankind is no longer under the Law, for the Law condemns. Rather, we are under grace (Romans 6:14), and can live by grace (1 Corinthians 15:10). We are to walk in the Spirit so that the righteous requirement of the Law would be fulfilled (Romans 7:6; 8:3,4,14).

The Apostle Paul makes it clear that since Jesus came, there is no distinction between Jew and Gentile – *all* people can be saved through faith in Jesus and be made righteous through Him (Romans 10:4,9-13). Jesus broke down the barrier between the Jew and Gentile, and the Law with all its strict ordinances. He brought peace and made it possible for us to become one in spirit and unity, redeemed by His blood (Ephesians 2:13-18).

The more a person tries to obey the Law in their own strength, the greater the frustration and realization of the power of sin. The only way to salvation is to appeal to the grace of God. In Paul's letter to Timothy, he explained how some of the teachers of the Law have strayed and do not understand what they teach. He said,

> *The purpose of the commandment is love from a pure heart, from a good conscience, and from sincere faith.... But we know the law is good if one uses it lawfully, knowing this: that the law is not made for a righteous person, but for the lawless and insubordinate, for the ungodly and for sinners...* (1 Timothy 1:5,8,9).

As believers in Jesus, who walk by the Spirit, we are children of God and made righteous through Him. The Old Testament Law is not binding upon us. Because of the redemption of Jesus, we can now enjoy, as James coined it, *"the perfect law of liberty"* (James 1:25) – a law full of mercy and grace.

Chapter 5

JESUS – THE MESSIAH

MESSIAH comes from the Hebrew word *Meshiach*, which means *Anointed One*. The Greek translation of this word is *Christos*. So when we say, *Jesus Christ*, we are in fact attaching His title of *Messiah* to His name and declaring that He is the Anointed One of God. In the Bible, when someone or something was anointed, it meant being set apart, or consecrated and sanctified for a specific task and purpose.

The kings of Judah and Israel were always anointed at their inauguration ceremony (Saul – 1 Samuel 10:1; David – 1 Samuel 16:12,13; 1 Kings 1:39,45; Solomon – 1 Kings 19:16). In fact, the expression, "*anointed of the Lord,*" was used synonymously with the title, *king* (1 Samuel 12:3,5; 24:6,10; 26:9,11,16,23; 2 Samuel 1:14,16; 19:21; Psalm 20:6). Priests were anointed for their service (Exodus 28:41; Leviticus 7:35,36; 10:7), as were some of the prophets (1 Kings 19:16; 1 Chronicles 16:22; Psalm 105:15). The tabernacle of Moses was anointed, showing its sanctification unto the Lord (Exodus 30:22-30; Leviticus 8:10-12; Numbers 7:1).

As prophesied, the Messiah would be One anointed by God Himself – anointed with the oil of gladness (Psalm 45:6; Hebrews 1:9). As God audibly declared, He was well pleased with His beloved Son. It was when the Holy Spirit came upon Jesus in the form of a dove on the occasion of His baptism that Jesus was anointed by God (Luke 3:22). The Messiah was empowered and set apart for His great task on earth to preach the Good News and to complete His work of redemption. He was anointed as Prophet, Priest, and King. In particular, the role of King was the main Messianic hope of the people. They expected their Messiah to be a powerful warrior King who would arise, bring deliverance, conquer their enemies, and bring back glory and independence to Israel.

These beliefs came from prophecies about the Messiah, but other prophecies concerning the Messiah are about His suffering, such as in Isaiah 53. Truly Jesus was the King; He was and is the King of kings. Many people followed Jesus and rightly believed Him to be the Messiah. The next logical step was to make Him King. In fact, the people had tried to forcibly do so (John 6:15), but they had their chronology wrong. Jesus tried to make them understand that His kingdom was not of this world (John 18:36). At His Second Coming, however, Jesus will fulfill the prophecies and return as a conquering King, be victorious over His enemies, and set up His kingdom. As the angels proclaimed,

> *The kingdoms of this world have become the kingdoms of our Lord and of His Christ, and He shall reign forever and ever!* (Revelation 11:15).

Messianic Prophecy

The sequence of events should not have been mistaken, for Daniel prophesied chronologically: first that Jerusalem would be rebuilt; then that in Jerusalem, the Messiah – anointed by the Holy One – would come to finish the transgression, put an end to sin, make reconciliation for iniquity, and bring in everlasting righteousness (Daniel 9:24).

Next in the order of Daniel's vision, the "*Messiah shall be cut off, but not for Himself*" (Daniel 9:26). It is true, Jesus died for the sins of the world. The next event is the destruction of the city of Jerusalem, which did in fact occur in 70 AD. Could it be any more specific than this? The only One who could fit these specific prophecies is Jesus! It is truly amazing! He fulfilled over 300 prophecies in detail. The odds of that occurring to anyone else are astronomical. **Prophecy then proves that Jesus is the Messiah.**

The Messiah Revealed

Throughout the Bible, many people testified and had the revelation that Jesus was the promised Messiah. Philip excitedly brought the news to Nathanael:

> *We have found Him of whom Moses in the law, and also the prophets, wrote – Jesus of Nazareth, the son of Joseph* (John 1:45).

And Nathanael, once he had an encounter with Jesus, testified: "*Rabbi, You are the Son of God! You are the King of Israel!*" (John 1:49). One of the strongest and most direct declarations was made by the Apostle Peter. He said, "*You are the Christ* [*Messiah*], *the Son of the living God*" (Matthew 16:16). Jesus was pleased and called Peter blessed, saying that God had revealed this truth to him. This same revelation was made known to many others as well, like Mary and Joseph, Elizabeth, the shepherds, Anna and Simeon (at the temple when Jesus was just a baby), John the Baptist, the disciples, and the Samaritan woman.

Names of Messiahship

Many referred to Jesus directly as the Messiah, and yet other names of Messiahship were also given to Him, such as:

- Saviour (Luke 2:10,11)
- Lamb of God (John 1:29)
- Son of God (Matthew 16:16; John 1:34,49)
- King of Israel (John 1:49)
- Son of David (Luke 18:38,39).

And even the demons knew who Jesus was and called Him:

- Holy One of God (Mark 1:24).

Jesus Claimed to be Messiah

Jesus Himself claimed to be the Messiah. When He first started His public ministry, He read in the synagogue from Isaiah 61 – a clear prophecy of the Messiah's duties and activities. He read aloud:

> *The Spirit of the Lord is upon Me, because He has anointed Me to preach the gospel to the poor. He has sent Me to heal the brokenhearted, to preach deliverance to the captives and recovery of sight to the blind, to set at liberty those who are oppressed, to preach the acceptable year of the Lord* (Luke 4:18,19).

Jesus announced that on the day He fulfilled them! (Luke 4:21). Indeed, all His claims, teachings, miracles, and everything He did, pointed to Him being the Messiah. Jesus said plainly to the Samaritan woman at the well that He was the Messiah. Also, He affirmed His deity by His wording, saying, *"I who speak to you am He."* Jesus referred to Himself as, *"I AM,"* the name of God (John 4:25,26).

When questioned by John the Baptist if He was "the Coming One," Jesus' answer proved that He fulfilled the Messianic prophecy of Isaiah (Isaiah 29:18,19; 35:4-6) – a prophecy that would have been familiar to John. Jesus said,

> *The blind receive their sight and the lame walk; the lepers are cleansed and the deaf hear; the dead are raised up and the poor have the gospel preached to them* (Matthew 11:3-5).

The people knew from the Old Testament that only the Messiah had the power and the right to heal the blind. Of all the miracles mentioned in the Old Testament, there is not one instance of healing the blind. This, in particular, was a sign of the Messiah which had spiritual significance. By this declaration, Jesus answered John positively and gave him sufficient evidence that He was indeed the Messiah.

Not only would the Messiah restore *physical* sight; but, even today, He gives *spiritual* sight to the blinded:

> *...whose minds the god of this age has blinded, who do not believe, lest the light of the gospel of the glory of Christ, who is the image of God, should shine on them.... For it is the God who commanded light to shine out of darkness who has shone in our hearts to give the light of the knowledge of the glory of God in the face of Jesus Christ* (2 Corinthians 4:4,6).

The risen and glorified Messiah, Jesus, appeared to Saul on the road to Damascus and commissioned him, saying, *"I now send you, to open their eyes and to turn them from darkness to light"* (Acts 26:17,18). When the light comes, the truth is revealed. Jesus is the Light of the World (John 8:12). Come to Him to find truth and life.

The Bible warns us about false prophets, false teachers, and false messiahs (Matthew 24:4,5). They are antichrists who deny the truth (1 John 2:18,22; 4:3; 2 John 7). They deny:

- Jesus is the Messiah
- the Father
- the incarnation of the Son – that Jesus, Yeshua, has come in the flesh, and thus...
- the deity of Jesus.

One day there will come an Antichrist – a man of evil, empowered by Satan, who will be false, deceive many, and will resist all the works of God (1 John 2:18). Peter cautions believers to *"be serious and watchful in your prayers"* (1 Peter 4:7). We are to read and study the Word of God, and abide in Jesus so we will not be deceived (1 John 2:24-27). The writings of the Gospel of Jesus are very important:

> *These are written that you may believe that Jesus is the Christ, the Son of God, and that believing you may have life in His name* (John 20:31).

The Messiahship of Jesus proves His deity, and His deity proves His Messiahship. When you confess and believe that Jesus is the Messiah, you are, in fact, endorsing the entire plan of God for the salvation of the world through Jesus. To affirm Jesus' Messiahship is to believe in the Father; the Son; and His incarnation, death, resurrection, and redemption.

In Peter's sermon to the Gentiles, he explained:

> *How God anointed Jesus of Nazareth with the Holy Spirit and with power, who went about doing good and healing all who were oppressed by the devil, for God was with Him. And we are witnesses of all things which He did.... To Him all the prophets witness that, through His name, whoever believes in Him will receive remission of sins* (Acts 10:38,39,43).

The Messiah's Purpose

The main purpose for the coming of the Messiah was for Jesus to fulfill God's plan for Him to be a Redeemer and a Saviour – One who would save the people from their sins. As the angel announced, *"For there is born to you this day in the city of David a Saviour, who is Christ the Lord"* (Luke 2:11). This spiritual salvation is much more necessary and more important than physical salvation. This is what the people hoped Jesus would do for them, by being their earthly King and overthrowing the Romans. What Jesus did for them, however, was far greater! He died in their place, and took the penalty of their sin upon Himself. He defeated Satan that they might have eternal life through faith in Him (Luke 24:46-48). When you believe in Jesus, the Messiah, you can be certain that you will see Him one day if you are:

> *...looking for the blessed hope and glorious appearing of our great God and Saviour Jesus Christ, who gave Himself for us, that He might redeem us from every lawless deed and purify for Himself His own special people...* (Titus 2:13,14).

Chapter 6

JESUS CHRIST – THE SON OF GOD

JESUS CHRIST has a distinct and unique relationship with God, the Father. The Bible refers to Jesus many times as the *Son of God*. The Son is a divine person in the Trinity. It is one of the revered names for our Lord Jesus. When we call Jesus the Son of God, it has deep theological and spiritual meaning. For some people who are not Christians, the use of the word *Son* can be misleading and misunderstood. It absolutely does not denote that God had a wife or a physical relationship with Mary. The thought of this is absurd and an insult to Christianity and to our Lord! It also does not mean that a son of God was created or born before eternity or creation, as believed by some of the old heathen religions. There is not one Christian in the whole world who thinks that when we say, *the Son of God*, it is in the physical sense. No, it is a spiritual and relational term.

The angel, who came to Mary to announce the coming of the Messiah, told her that she would have a Son and that

He *"will be called the Son of the Highest"* (Luke 1:32). Mary needed an explanation and asked how this could happen since she was a virgin, and the angel told her:

> *The Holy Spirit will come upon you, and the power of the Highest will overshadow you; therefore, also, that Holy One who is to be born will be called the Son of God.... For with God nothing will be impossible* (Luke 1:35,37).

Jesus, then, had no earthly, natural father. Joseph, the man Mary was engaged to at the time of the divine visitation and miraculous conception, treated Jesus as a son. However, Jesus was not his physical son. An angel also revealed news of this miraculous conception to Joseph, otherwise he would have broken off the engagement with Mary. For in that culture, if a girl was found to be pregnant before marriage, she could be stoned to death. Joseph, however, knew that Mary's pregnancy and Jesus' birth came as a direct result of God's power and intervention.

Jesus was born to the virgin Mary. He was given to the world as a gift from God for our salvation. About 700 years before His birth, the prophet Isaiah wrote of this great gift from God: *"For unto us a Child is born, unto us a Son is given..."* (Isaiah 9:6). At the right time in history, when God had ordained it, Jesus was sent into the world. In Galatians 4:4, we read, *"But when the fullness of the time had come, God sent forth His Son, born of a woman...."* Isaiah also prophesied, *"Behold, the virgin shall conceive and bear a Son, and shall call His name Immanuel"* (Isaiah 7:14). Matthew quoted this verse and explained that *Immanuel* means *"God with us"* (Matthew 1:23). There are other Old Testament prophesies that also speak of the Son of God

(Psalm 2:7,12; Proverbs 30:4).

Jesus' disciples recognized His special relationship to God. Nathanael testified that He was the Son of God, as did Peter (John 1:49; 6:69). The Roman centurion at the foot of the cross watched all that had happened to Jesus and testified that He was the Son of God. Angels of God confess Him to be the Son, as do the demons.

The Apostle Paul, while teaching about God's goodness and salvation, called Jesus *"the Son of His love"* (Colossians 1:13), for in sending Jesus, it was the greatest expression of God's love for us. Jesus is also called *"the Son of the Father"* by the beloved disciple, John (2 John 3), who also in his gospel and epistles makes reference five times to Jesus being the ***only*** Son. The famous Scripture in John 3:16, tells us that God *"gave His only begotten Son"* – words that express the uniqueness of Jesus. In fact, 40 times the word *Son* is related to God using the personal pronoun His Son. God Himself several times called Jesus, *"My Son"* or *"My beloved Son."*

Jesus affirmed this unique relationship with God many times by calling Him, *"My Father"* (John 5:17), again using the personal pronoun instead of saying, as other people would say, "our Father." The religious leaders who were against Jesus understood His words to be blasphemous, as the Apostle John explains:

> *Therefore the Jews sought all the more to kill Him, because He...said that God was His Father, making Himself equal with God* (John 5:18).

Of course it was not blasphemy, since it was true, for Jesus confirmed many times His equality with God (John 5:19-30). Jesus expressed His divine, eternal Sonship by saying, *"And now, O Father, glorify Me together with Yourself, with the glory which I had with You before the world was"* (John 17:5). Jesus also affirmed His oneness with God, the Father, in His prayer for those who believe in Him to be unified, by saying, *"...that they all may be one, as You, Father, are in Me, and I in You"* (John 17:21; John 10:30-38). The Apostle Paul declares, *"Great is the mystery of godliness: God was manifested in the flesh...*(1 Timothy 3:16).

Some might argue that other people in the Bible are called sons of God or referred to as a son of God. In the New Testament, believers are called children or sons of God (John 1:12; 1 John 3:1,2; Galatians 3:6). Notice that in these cases, when speaking of anyone other than Jesus, it is always in the plural, or with the little word "a" in front of the word son: He is *a* son of God. But with reference to Jesus, it is always very special. By saying He is *the* Son or *the only* Son, gives distinction and greater and more specific meaning.

Why is Jesus called *the Son of God?*

1. **The Son reveals the nature of the Father.** Jesus – by His Word, deeds, example, nature, character, and qualities – reveals the nature, character, and attributes of God. More often than not, a son is very much like his father. Jesus knows the Father, even more intimately than any person could know any other person. Jesus teaches us about God, who God is, along with His plan and purpose for our lives. You cannot see God, nor know Him, except through the Son (Matthew 11:27).

2. **The Son reveals the image of God, the Father.** Paul says of Jesus that *"He is the image of the invisible God"* (Colossians 1:15), and the writer to the Hebrews affirms

that God has spoken to us through Jesus who is *"the express image of His person"* (Hebrews 1:3). Jesus said, *"He who has seen Me has seen the Father..."* (John 14:9,11; Philippians 2:6; John 1:18). Jesus is the very essence of God. He is all of God (John 10:30,33). He has all the glories of deity, all the authority, power, works, and claims of God. It is a unique and divine union.

3. **The Son reveals the glory of the Father.** Often when a son is a great person or has accomplished something great, credit is given to his father. I used to live in Brantford, Ontario, where I often heard about a person who grew up there, known as "the great one," namely Wayne Gretzky. But I also heard about his father, who was given much credit for Wayne's success by teaching him to skate and play hockey, and by placing him on teams. So the success of the son brings honour to the father. The wonderful deeds of Jesus were all done to bring glory to God. Jesus said, *"And whatever you ask in My name, that I will do, that the Father may be glorified in the Son"* (John 14:13).

   When we have answers to prayer, be sure to give glory to God. We learn in 2 Corinthians 4:6 that God has brought those who believe out of darkness *"to give the light of the knowledge of the glory of God in the face of Jesus Christ."* Another name of great importance, like the Son, that is given to Jesus is *the Word*, or *Logos*, which expresses the mind, will, and glorious person of God, as well as the unity of the Son and the Father. Scripture records this truth:

In the beginning was the Word, and the Word was with God, and the Word was God.... And the Word became flesh and dwelt among us, and we beheld His glory, the glory as of the only begotten of the Father, full of grace and truth (John 1:1,14).

4. **He has come from God and is not of this world.** Although He came in the flesh, Jesus is not tainted with our earthly, inherited, sinful nature. He is the Holy One who came from above.

5. **It expresses the unique and eternal love of God, the Father, toward Jesus.** God audibly declared Jesus to be His beloved Son. Jesus Himself said, *"For the Father loves the Son"* (John 5:20) and *"for you loved Me before the foundation of the world"* (John 17:24; cf. Colossians 1:13; 2 John 3). The love of God is expressed through Jesus, who prayed for all believers *"that the love with which You loved Me may be in them, and I in them"* (John 17:26). When we have accepted Jesus into our hearts, His love fills our being.

6. **To describe His divine position.** An only son of a great man is given the same honour as the father, and all that the father has is, in effect, the son's. Jesus is worthy of all the honour and glory that is due God:

   All should honour the Son just as they honour the Father. He who does not honour the Son does not honour the Father who sent Him (John 5:23; 1 John 2:23).

Let us give honour to Jesus today! Belief in the Son is the foundation of our faith. To state, "Jesus is the Son of God" is a divinely revealed declaration of faith in Him, as Peter said to Jesus, *"You are the Christ, the Son of the living God"* (John 6:69; Matthew 16:16). Belief in the Son decides our destiny.

> *He who believes in the Son has everlasting life; and he who does not believe the Son shall not see life, but the wrath of God abides on him* (John 3:36; John 3:16,17).

We all want to please God and have His divine favour. When we believe that Jesus is the Son of God, it is not only pleasing to God, but absolutely vital for eternal life in heaven with Him.

It is the spirit of antichrist that denies Jesus as the Son of God. In Scripture, we read:

> *Who is a liar but he who denies that Jesus is the Christ? He is antichrist who denies the Father and the Son. Whoever denies the Son does not have the Father either; he who acknowledges the Son has the Father also* (1 John 2:22,23).

Do you want to be close to God and have a genuine relationship with Him? Then please open your heart, ask God to reveal to you the truth, and believe in the Lord Jesus Christ.

Our faith in the Son of God will defeat Satan and triumph over the evil influences of this world. "*Who is he who overcomes the world, but he who believes that Jesus is the Son of God?*" (1 John 5:5). Also in Scripture, we learn that the Son of God was manifested in the flesh "*that He might destroy the works of the devil*" (1 John 3:8). When Jesus died on the cross and was resurrected, He was victorious over sin and Satan. We, by belief in Him, the Son of God, can share in His victory and become beloved children of God! (Romans 1:3-6).

Believers in Jesus need to pray for those who are spiritually blind, that their eyes would be opened, so that they might know whom Jesus really is. Like the blind man who was healed physically and, most importantly, spiritually, for he came to believe in Jesus as the Son of God. Jesus asked him:

> *"Do you believe in the Son of God?" He answered and said, "Who is He, Lord, that I may believe in Him?" And Jesus said to him, "You have both seen Him and it is He who is talking with you." Then he said, "Lord, I believe!" And he worshipped Him* (John 9:35-38).

Believe with your whole heart that Jesus is the Son of God and worship Him, for He is worthy of our praise!

Chapter 7

Jesus Christ – the Creator

ONE OF the unique aspects of Christianity is our belief and Scriptural affirmation that Jesus Christ is the Creator of all things. Some people believe that Jesus is only a prophet, but does a prophet have the power to create? Would God give a mere man one of His most personal and inherent abilities? No, creation is only possible by God alone.

In the creation account, found in the book of Genesis, we read: *"In the beginning God created the heavens and the earth"* (Genesis 1:1). The Hebrew word for God is *Elohim*, a plural word. The triune God – the Father, the pre-incarnate Son, and the Holy Spirit – were all active in creation. *"Then God said, 'Let Us make man in Our image, according to Our likeness'"*(Genesis 1:26).

In the New Testament, we read words echoing the Genesis account of creation: *"In the beginning was the Word, and the Word was with God, and the Word was God"* (John 1:1). Jesus was the Word who became flesh

(John 1:14). Scripture continues:

> *He was in the beginning with God. All things were made through Him, and without Him nothing was made that was made* (John 1:2,3).

Jesus was the cause of all creation. He was the source for all life. There would be nothing without Jesus. We read in Scripture:

> *For by Him all things were created that are in heaven and that are on earth, visible and invisible.... All things were created through Him and for Him. And He is before all things, and in Him all things consist* (Colossians 1:16,17).

The eternal Lord Jesus has created for Himself everything material and immaterial. The greatness and extent of His creation is beyond our comprehension. Scientists are still today discovering new things, both here on earth and in the universe.

Our Lord's creation is truly immeasurable. Everything created has been ordained for His glory and to praise Him (Isaiah 43:7; Psalm 148). When sin entered the world through Adam, a darkness came into the world; and His wonderful creation, which He declared to be "*good*" (Genesis 1:31), is presently groaning under the influence of sin. There will come a glorious day, however, when Jesus will bring final deliverance to all (Romans 8:18-23), after Satan and his cohorts are thrown into the Lake of Fire (Revelation 20:10,14,15). Our Lord Jesus will "*make all things new*" (Revelation 21:5), and reign supremely over all. What a glorious and joyous day that will be for all creation. Until that day of freedom, Jesus is at work sustaining all creation. Without Him, there would be no life, only chaos and emptiness.

The writer to the Hebrews said that God...

> *...has in these last days spoken to us by His Son, whom He has appointed heir of all things, through whom also He made the worlds; who being the brightness of His glory and the express image of His person, and upholding all things by the word of His power, when He had by Himself purged our sins, sat down at the right hand of the Majesty on high* (Hebrews 1:2,3; cf. John 17:5).

Jesus is the Almighty. By His word everything came into being (Psalm 33:6,9). By His word He created that which is formed from that which was not:

> *By faith we understand that the worlds were framed by the word of God, so that the things which are seen were not made of things which are visible* (Hebrews 11:3).

By His word, all creation is sustained and continues to exist.

In heaven, our Almighty God is praised. In John's vision he heard the glorious hymn of the heavenly congregation, singing to the Creator who sits on the throne:

> *You are worthy, O Lord, to receive glory and honour and power; for You created all things, and by Your will they exist and were created* (Revelation 4:11).

Creation bears witness to the glory and power of God. There have been some people who have come to know the Lord after first considering the majesty of creation. King

David sang, "*The heavens declare the glory of God; and the firmament shows His handiwork*" (Psalm 19:1).

One of the reasons that Jesus came into the world was to bring glory to God and to reveal Him – this He also did in creation. Paul wrote,

> *For since the creation of the world His invisible attributes are clearly seen, being understood by the things that are made, even His eternal power and Godhead, so that they are without excuse* (Romans 1:20).

When people worship that which has been created and not the Creator Himself, they are without excuse. Paul states that they have fallen into sin, and the wrath and judgement of God is upon them (Romans 1:25; 2:5).

Yet Jesus brings deliverance from the power of sin. He also gives new life. John continued his discourse of Jesus, the Creator, saying, "*In Him was life, and the life was the light of men*" (John 1:4). He is the Light (cf. John 1:7-9). There can be no life without light, just as there can be no life without Jesus. The Lord said, "*I am the light of the world. He who follows Me shall not walk in darkness, but have the light of life*" (John 8:12). That means Jesus gives life to those who believe in Him – abundant life in the present and everlasting life in the future. He has made each believer a "*new creation*" (2 Corinthians 5:17; Psalm 102:18) by transforming from within, renewing and making alive one's spirit. Paul told the Colossians to put carnality to death and "*to put on the new man who is renewed in knowledge according to the image of Him who created him*" (Colossians 3:10). Yes, Jesus brings restoration to our souls and has given us new spiritual life! "*For in Him we live and move and have our being"* (Acts 17:28; cf. 1 Corinthians 8:6).

Jesus Himself said,

> *I am the Alpha and the Omega, the Beginning and the End...who is and who was and who is to come, the Almighty* (Revelation 1:8).

And again He declared, *"I am the Alpha and the Omega, the First and the Last"* (Revelation 1:11). The great thinker and author, the late Charles Rolls, wrote an insightful series of books on the names and titles of Jesus Christ. Concerning the name *"Alpha and Omega,"* he wrote,

> I am convinced that no mind is big enough to comprehend the magnitude of the measureless range of dignity and glory embodied in such a stupendous claim (Charles J. Rolls, *The Indescribable Christ*, Loizeaux Brothers, Inc., Neptune, New Jersey: 1983, pg. 16).

The prophet Isaiah recorded the rebuke of the Lord to the sinful children of Israel, wherein He insisted that they listen and heed His words. The Lord declared:

> *I am He, I am the First, I am also the Last. Indeed My hand has laid the foundation of the earth, and My right hand has stretched out the heavens* (Isaiah 48:12,13).

Clearly, the Lord who is speaking is Jesus, the Son. He continues with these words:

> *From the time that it was, I was there. And now the Lord God and His Spirit have sent Me. Thus says the Lord, your Redeemer, the Holy One of Israel; I*

am the Lord your God, who teaches you to profit, who leads you in the way you should go (Isaiah 48:16,17; cf. 41:4; Proverbs 8:22-31).

Oh, doesn't the Lord Jesus deserve our praise and adoration. He not only created us, but shows us how to live by His words and example. As we look at His glorious life on earth, there are many instances when **He proved Himself to be the Great Creator:**

- **He changed the water into wine**, thus creating something new (John 2:1-11).
- **He multiplied a small amount of food** on two separate occasions to feed thousands (John 6).
- **He created new eyes** from mud (John 9; Mark 8).
- **He had authority over nature** and controls His creation. For He calmed the sea and walked upon it, and caused the fish to have the coin in its mouth so He and Peter could pay the temple tax (Matthew 17:27).
- **He gave life to the physically dead.**
- **He gave life to the spiritually dead**, making a new creation.

It is something truly amazing that the Great Creator of everything would consider humankind. King David commented, "*What is man, that you are mindful of him?*" (Psalm 8:4). How marvellous, and what a great expression of God's love! He became a man and submitted Himself even to the point of death on the cross. Humankind would finally have redemption, being purchased by His precious blood that was shed to deliver you and me from sin and darkness. Indeed, Jesus is preparing a place for the redeemed – a place with Him in glory (John 14:2,3). He will create a new heaven and a new earth, for there will come a day when that which He created in the beginning will eventually pass away (2 Peter 3:3-7,11; Revelation 21:1), but the new creation will abide forever (Revelation 2:5). Hallelujah! Are you a new creation in Christ? Believe on the Lord Jesus and you will be saved!

Chapter 8

JESUS CHRIST – THE LIFE-GIVER

OUR LORD and Saviour Jesus Christ is the Life-Giver. He said, *"I am the resurrection and the life"* (John 11:25; 1 Corinthians 15:22). He always proved the truth of His words by His deeds. He proved Himself the Almighty Life-Giver with divine authority and divine power, by raising the dead to life. This was one of the unique features of His earthly ministry. Only God can restore life to that which was dead. In chapter 7, we looked at Scriptural proof that Jesus is the Creator of all things. He, who is the Creator, surely also has the power to give life. We read in Scripture, *"In Him was life, and the life was the light of men"* (John 1:4). Jesus is the source of life. He is the fountain of life. In fact, He is the life of life itself. Jesus said, *"For as the Father has life in Himself, so He has granted the Son to have life in Himself"* (John 5:26).

The fact that Jesus raised the dead was proof that He was the Messiah. When John the Baptist questioned if Jesus was the *"Coming One,"* the response from Jesus was, *"Go and tell John the things you have seen and heard."* Among those things listed was, *"the dead are raised"* (Luke 7:22). It was foretold that the Messiah would heal the broken-hearted and comfort those in mourning (cf. Isaiah 61:1,2; Luke 4:18). Truly, Jesus brought much joy and celebration to the funerals of those He raised to life!

In the first recorded instance, Jesus brought to life the only son of a widow in Nain, a town traditionally located just southeast of Nazareth. At the divinely appointed time, Jesus entered with the joyous crowd following Him, just as the mournful crowd was leaving town to go to the graveyard. Jesus had compassion on the weeping mother and, by the power of His word, commanded, *"Young man, I say to you, arise"* (Luke 7:14). The dead man lying upon the open coffin, which was like a stretcher, came to life, sat up and began to speak! The mournful crowd became a joyous crowd. They proclaimed, *"God has visited His people"* (Luke 7:16).

The second incident was also the raising of an only child. It occurred shortly after the death of a 12-year-old girl whose father, Jairus, was a ruler of the synagogue in Capernaum, a town on the shore of the Sea of Galilee. Jairus had faith that Jesus could heal his daughter. Again, by the power of His spoken word, *"Little girl, I say to you, arise"* (Mark 5:41), the child's spirit returned to her, she stood up and began walking around.

The third recorded resurrection from death to life was shortly before Jesus' arrest and crucifixion. It occurred in Bethany, a town just to the east of Jerusalem, on the eastern slope of the Mount of Olives. The man was Lazarus, the only brother of Mary and Martha. In John's account, we are given many specific details of this event. Jesus had heard of Lazarus' sickness and was summoned to come, but He purposefully delayed His coming. He had a plan. It was to raise Lazarus from death *"for the glory of God, that the Son of God may be glorified through it"* (John 11:4).

By the time Jesus arrived in Bethany, Lazarus had been in the grave for four days. His sisters lamented that if Jesus had arrived earlier, He could have done something. Jesus assured Martha, *"Your brother will rise again"* (John 11:23). She understood this to mean the final resurrection day, but Jesus revealed to Martha that He had the power to bring resurrection in the present day as well. It is here that Jesus made the great claim: *"I am the resurrection and the life. He who believes in Me, though he may die, he shall live"* (John 11:25).

We see the tender heart of Jesus and His humanity in that He wept with the bereaved women, and we also see His awesome divine power. Again, at Jesus' command, *"Lazarus, come forth!"* (John 11:43), the resurrection power of Jesus was manifested. I have heard it said that if Jesus had not specified the man by name, then all the dead at the cemetery could have arisen. What a sight that would have been!

Even with the undisputed miracle of Lazarus' resurrection, the religious leaders would not believe in Jesus. But many other people did believe, and news of the miracle began to spread. The raising of Lazarus was the climactic event in Jesus' public ministry. It prompted the quick assembly of the Sanhedrin (a group of ruling men) who then decided to have Jesus killed as soon as possible, just before the significant Passover when the children of Israel celebrated God's deliverance from bondage. Everything happened in the plan and purpose of God.

Of course, the greatest resurrection we read of in the New Testament is the resurrection of Jesus Himself, by His own inherent power. It was God's will for Jesus to die that He might become our Passover Lamb. It was God's will for Him to come to life again on the third day. Jesus *is* alive and is interceding on our behalf before God. He arose victorious over the grave, over death, and over Satan. He arose with a new glorified body. Interestingly, at the same time as Jesus' death and resurrection, when His blood had purchased redemption, there was such power, spiritual authority, and victory over Satan, that even some of the righteous people who had previously died in Jerusalem, were raised to life again (Matthew 27:51-53).

In the Old Testament, there are three stories of resurrection by the power of God. They involved the great prophets, Elijah and Elisha; and in these instances, the resurrections brought honour to the man of God (1 Kings 17:17-24; 2 Kings 4:8-37; 13:20,21).

When Jesus raised the dead, it was a testimony to many that Jesus truly was the Son of God and that His claims were true. He also gave His disciples the authority to do miracles – including raising the dead – in His name (Matthew 10:7,8; Mark 16:15-18). We read of Peter in Jaffa, who raised Tabitha to life (Acts 9:36-42); and we read of Paul, who with the authority of Jesus, raised to life the young man in Asia (Acts 20:9-12).

In summary, what have we learned about the Life-Giver? Why did Jesus raise the dead? It has deep spiritual meaning. He did so:

- as a proof of His deity
- to reveal God's glory

- to reveal the glory of the Son
- to cause people to believe
- to prove His Messiahship
- to reveal His authority and sovereign power
- to verify the truthfulness of His calling and divine mission
- to give credibility to His claims and integrity to His teaching
- to show His great love and compassion.

Jesus Gives Spiritual Life

Most importantly, Jesus, the Life-Giver, gives us spiritual life and life everlasting. Of the believer in Jesus, it is written:

> *And you He made alive, who were dead in trespasses and sins.... But God, who is rich in mercy, because of His great love...made us alive together with Christ (by grace you have been saved), and raised us up together, and made us sit together in the heavenly places in Christ Jesus* (Ephesians 2:1,4-6; cf. Col 2:13; John 5:24,25).

Our Christian faith is based upon a blessed hope of glory (Colossians 1:27; Philippians 1:20-24; 3:10-14; 1 John 3:1-3). We hope in our living Lord Jesus and the fact that we, too, will one day be alive with Him forevermore (2 Corinthians 5:6-8; 1 Thessalonians 4:13-17). When we know the Lord by faith, and have asked Him to forgive us our sins, we do not need to fear death (Hebrews 2:14,15). Through Jesus Christ, *"we are more than conquerors"* (Romans 8:37; 2 Timothy 1:10). Through Him we have all we need, be it for life, for death, or for eternity.

Christianity stands unique and supreme above any religion, for it is centred in a living Person – the Lord Jesus Christ – who has the power to transform and give life. Do you want assurance of salvation and everlasting life? Only Jesus can give that to us. Would you put your faith in Him today? It will be the best decision of your life.

Chapter 9

JESUS CHRIST – THE SIGHT-GIVER

EARLIER, we studied about Jesus being a miracle worker, the Life-Giver, and the Creator. Now I want to expand upon the great and miraculous work of the Lord Jesus in bringing sight to the blind. It is yet another feature which makes Jesus Christ unique and supreme. The miracle of sight-giving or sight restoration is very significant, for not only did Jesus heal physical blindness but, more importantly, He healed spiritual blindness. Jesus claimed to be *"the True Light."* He is the Source of light, the Creator of light, and the Giver of light.

Why does healing blinded eyes make Jesus unique and why is it significant?

1. **It is the prophesied work of the Messiah alone.** With all the many miracles in the Old Testament, there is not one instance of blind eyes being healed. It was common knowledge among the Jews that only the Messiah could

restore sight. It was a sign of the ushering in of a new Messianic era. The prophet Isaiah foretold about this glorious coming era: *"Then the eyes of the blind shall be opened"* (Isaiah 35:5). When Jesus began His public ministry, He read from one of Isaiah's Messianic prophesies about the Messiah restoring sight to the blind, and He claimed to fulfill it (Luke 4:18). When John the Baptist was in prison, he sent his followers to ask Jesus if He was the Promised Messiah. Jesus affirmed their question by saying, *"Go and tell John the things which you hear and see."* And the first statement He made to affirm it was, *"The blind receive their sight..."* (Matthew 11:3-5).

2. **Only God can make new eyes and give them sight.** Jesus showed His divine creative work in making new eyes for the man who had been born blind. A whole chapter of the book of John is devoted to this story. The healed man rightly testified,

   Since the world began it has been unheard of that anyone opened the eyes of one who was born blind. If this Man were not from God, He could do nothing (John 9:32,33; 10:21).

   The New Testament recorded that Jesus healed seven blind people (Matthew 9:27; 12:22; 20:30; Mark 8:22; John 9:1), but there were likely many more who received sight, for we read that wherever Jesus went, He healed many people (Matthew 4:23; 8:16). The Apostle John tells us that if he mentioned everything that Jesus did, then the whole world could not contain the books (John 21:25; 20:30,31).

3. **Jesus healed the blind to express His love** and compassion for people. Physical eyesight is not a necessity to life, but it certainly is a wonderful blessing. Many blind people today have quite normal lives and accomplish much; but in that ancient Jewish culture, a blind person had to resort to begging for his livelihood. Most people looked down on them and considered their blindness a punishment from God for sin (John 9:1-3). When Jesus passed by – *"the Sun of Righteousness...with healing in His wings"* (Malachi 4:2) – these blind people called out to Him in desperate need, *"have mercy"* (Matthew 9:27; 20:30). In every case, Jesus responded with compassion. He healed them as a display of God's love, mercy, power, glory, and authority.

4. **Jesus gave His disciples His own divine authority to heal the blind.** He commissioned His followers and sent them out to preach and heal the sick. He said they would do things just as He did, and surely this included the healing of blinded eyes (John 14:12). We read in the book of Acts that the apostles and other followers of Jesus did great miracles in His name (Acts 2:43; 5:12-16; 8:5-7,13; 19:11,12). For example, the Lord struck Saul with blindness for three days; but when Ananias, a righteous follower of Jesus laid hands on him and prayed, Saul's sight was restored (Acts 9:17). Saul became the Apostle Paul, who not only experienced Jesus' healing, but also came to believe in Jesus and see the truth. Jesus commissioned him to go to the Gentiles,

> *...to open their eyes and to turn them from darkness to light, and from the power of Satan to God, that they may receive forgiveness of sins and an*

inheritance among those who are sanctified by faith... (Acts 26:18).

5. **The healing of the physically blind symbolized the healing of the spiritually blind and salvation from sin and darkness.** Isaiah not only prophesied that the Messiah would give sight to the blind, but also sight to the spiritually blind:

   In that day the deaf shall hear the words of the book, and the eyes of the blind shall see out of obscurity and out of darkness (Isaiah 29:18).

   The healed man who had been blind since birth also received a more important healing – that of spiritual sight and salvation (Isaiah 49:6; Luke 2:30-32), for he came to believe in Jesus (John 9:38-41). The religious Jews had judged him as sinful since he had been born blind, but Jesus rebuked them, saying,

   For judgement I have come into this world, that those who do not see may see, and that those who see may be made blind (John 9:39).

   Those who do not believe in Jesus are spiritually blind (John 3:17-21). He called the hypocritical religious leaders *"blind guides"* (Matthew 23:16; 15:14) since they lived in darkness and did not know the truth.

6. **The healing of the physically blind proved Jesus' claim of being the *"Light of the world"*** (John 8:12) – a clear claim of divinity. He opened eyes and brought light to people who had lived in darkness. In the same way, He saves people from sin and proves Himself to be the Light and to give life (2 Timothy 1:10). There

can be no life without the Light. Nothing would exist without Jesus. He is the Creator (John 1:3). Isaiah prophesied,

The people who walked in darkness have seen a great light; those who dwelt in the land of the shadow of death, upon them a light has shined (Isaiah 9:2).

The Apostle John especially emphasized that Jesus is the Light. He quoted Jesus as saying, *"I have come as a light into the world, that whoever believes in Me should not abide in darkness"* (John 12:46; 12:36; 1:4,5,7,9; 3:19-21). The Psalmist understood this truth: *"For with You is the fountain of life; in Your light we see light"* (Psalm 36:9; 146:8). There will come a day when Jesus Himself will literally be the Light. In the book of Revelation, we read a prophetic description of the new Jerusalem:

And the city had no need of the sun or of the moon to shine in it, for the glory of God illuminated it, and the Lamb is its light. And the nations of those who are saved shall walk in its light (Revelation 21:23,24; Isaiah 60:1-3).

7. **Jesus brought light that believers might likewise be light,** overcome temptations, and ultimately defeat Satan. As the Light, Jesus revealed the nature and glory of God. Believers in Jesus, who now shine as lights for Him, must likewise, by word and deed, bring glory to God. In Scripture, we read:

You are...His own special people, that you may proclaim the praises of Him who called you out of darkness into His marvellous light (1 Peter 2:9).

> Jesus also tells His people, "*You are the light of the world.... Let your light shine...*" (Matthew 5:14-16). And we read in the book of Philippians,
>
> *For it is God who works in you...that you may become blameless and harmless, children of God without fault in the midst of a crooked and perverse generation, among whom you shine as lights in the world* (Philippians 2:13-15).
>
> The people of God are citizens in the kingdom of light (Colossians 1:13) and, therefore, we are in constant spiritual warfare against the kingdom of darkness (Ephesians 6:12).

Truly, our Lord Jesus is the Sight-Giver. He is Light and Life. Without Him, our understanding is darkened, and we live in ignorance and sin (Ephesians 4:18). But with Him, when we make Him our Saviour and Lord, the eyes of our understanding are enlightened (Ephesians 1:18). We become light and we walk as children of the light (Ephesians 5:8-14; 1 John 1:5-7; 2:8-11). Our walk in the light must reflect Jesus and be modelled after Him. If we walk in the light, we will be victorious over temptation, sin, and even over Satan and his demons. For wherever there is light, there can be no darkness (John 1:5). As children in the kingdom of light, we are to be transparent, and our testimony will have great influence.

When we live in the light, we combat the darkness of Satan who causes spiritual blindness. The Apostle Paul explained:

> *But even if our gospel is veiled, it is veiled to those who are perishing, whose minds the god of this age*

> *has blinded, who do not believe, lest the light of the gospel of the glory of Christ, who is the image of God, should shine on them* (2 Corinthians 4:3,4).

It is the divine work of Jesus that gives us sight and brings light. Paul continued,

> *For it is the God who commanded light to shine out of darkness who has shone in our hearts to give the light of the knowledge of the glory of God in the face of Jesus Christ* (2 Corinthians 4:6; Hebrews 1:3).

It is through the Word of God that we receive illumination. Pray as the psalmist, *"Open my eyes, that I may see wondrous things"* (Psalm 119:18,105,130; 2 Peter 1:19). Jesus is willing to give you spiritual sight for He is Light and the Way of salvation (Psalm 27:1).

Chapter 10

The Authority of Jesus Christ

ALL THE words of Jesus were spoken with great authority, and all the actions of Jesus were done with equal authority. He had a divine calling, a divine purpose, and a divine anointing from above, for He came from heaven above (Luke 4:17,18; John 3:13,31). He even explained to His followers, *"All authority has been given to Me in heaven and on earth"* (Matthew 28:18; John 3:35). It was clear to all that Jesus was a Man of authority, which made Him unique. His disciples and all who listened to Him constantly marvelled at His authority and power (Mark 1:22; Luke 4:32).

After Jesus had displayed His authority by clearing the temple of the dishonest merchants, the religious hypocrites asked Him, *"By what authority are You doing these things? And who gave You this authority?"* (Matthew 21:23). Jesus wouldn't answer them directly because He knew their motives were evil and that they were trying to trap Him. Instead, Jesus responded with the parable of the landowner who sent servants to collect his rightful share of the profit. Those to whom he had leased the vineyard refused to give the owner what was rightfully his, and they killed his servants. Finally, he sent his son, for surely they would obey him, as he had all the authority of his father. They refused and, likewise, killed the son.

When the religious hypocrites realized the parable was about them and their rejection of Jesus, it made them very angry. Jesus was telling them that even though He clearly had the right and authority of God, they still did not listen to Him and would, therefore, suffer judgement and punishment (Matthew 21:23-46). It was a strong warning to repent, believe in Jesus, and accept His divine authority. Sadly, they did not repent, but rather tried to find a way to kill Jesus. When their own soldiers had been sent out to arrest Him, they returned without Him, saying, *"No man ever spoke like this Man!"* (John 7:46; Mark 6:2).

Jesus Has Innate Authority

Jesus' authority is a part of His very nature and it is inherently and rightfully His because of who He is – the eternal Son of God. Even when He was 12 years old, His authority was evident and He astonished the teachers of the Law at the temple in Jerusalem (Luke 2:47). Although Jesus was meek and humble, this did not mean that He was weak or a "pushover." No, meekness meant that Jesus had strength and power under control.

The people all sensed that, while in His presence, they were in the presence of a King. Jesus gave commands. He uttered strong rebukes and made authoritative claims; claims that only God could make: *"I am the Way, the Truth and the Life"* (John 14:6). He had majestic dignity and showed no fear, even when He stood before Pilate, who had the power to condemn Him to death (John 18:36,37). Jesus responded to the magistrate, *"You could have no power [authority] at all against Me unless it had been given you from above"* (John 19:11). As the all-authoritative God, Jesus accepted worship and He forgave sin.

Jesus Earned His Authority

Not only was Jesus' authority innate, but He also earned it. First, by living a perfect, holy, and sinless life. He asserted, *"Which of you convicts Me of sin?"* (John 8:46). Of course, no one could truthfully convict Jesus of any wrong. Second, by completing God's divine plan of redemption. His death on the cross, His glorious resurrection and ascension, gave Him the right to officially rule and reign as King, to be the highly exalted Lord (Philippians 2:8-11; Acts 2:36), and also the Great High Priest (Hebrews 4:14-16; 17:25,26).

In Romans 1:3, we read that Jesus was:

> *...declared to be the Son of God with power, according to the Spirit of holiness, by the resurrection from the dead....*

He accomplished a marvellous work by being the substitutionary sacrifice. Yes, Jesus paid the price for sin, taking our punishment upon Himself. He suffered and died in our place that we might have everlasting life. Can you imagine the all-powerful, all-authoritative God of the universe, humbling Himself even to death on a cursed cross because of His great love for you and me? Oh, I thank Jesus for the wonderful redemption from sin and death that He has given us! He certainly deserves all the glory, honour, and praise!

How did Jesus display His authority?

1. **In His teaching.** After His great Sermon on the Mount, we read in Scripture, *"...the people were astonished at His teaching, for He taught them as one having authority, and not as the scribes"* (Matthew 7:28,29; Luke 4:32). In this sermon, Jesus said repeatedly, *"You have heard it said...but I say to you,"* thus showing that His words superceded that of all earthly authority.

2. **He forgave sin,** a divine prerogative alone. Jesus said of Himself, *"the Son of Man has power* [or *authority*] *on earth to forgive sins"* (Matthew 9:6); and He even forgave the woman caught in adultery, saying, *"Neither do I condemn you; go and sin no more"* (John 8:11).

3. **Through miracles.** He healed every kind of sickness with His own power and with the word of authority (Mark 1:34; Matthew 8:1-17). His miracles caused the people to be in awe of God and to give Him the glory He deserves. Jesus even gave His disciples the authority to heal and perform great miracles in His name, which they did as recorded in Scripture (Matthew 10:1).

4. **Over nature.** Surely the Creator of all is Lord of all. He calmed the raging sea by merely speaking the words, *"Peace, be still!"* (Mark 4:39). His disciples were fearful and exclaimed, *"Who can this be, that even the wind and the sea obey Him!"* (Mark 4:41). Jesus also calmed the fearful human nature, and brought peace. He even had control over the fish in the sea. On two different occasions, He caused fish to go in the nets of His disciples, and He provided the temple tax that He and Peter required from the mouth of a fish. To serve as an object

lesson, Jesus cursed a fig tree, and with just His words, He caused the tree to wither and die (Mark 11:12-14,20,21).

5. **Over death.** He raised the dead to life with just a word. He also displayed authority over His own death. He said, *"I have power to lay it down, and I have power* [*or authority*] *to take it again"* (John 10:18). The grave could not keep Him, for after three days in the tomb, He arose, just as He said He would!

6. **Over Satan.** He freed people from bondage to Satan, which was an important part of His ministry on earth (John 10:10; 8:34-36; Hebrews 2:14,15; Luke 19:10). He cast out many demons and had authority over them (Matthew 8:16). He was manifested to destroy the works of Satan (1 John 3:8). In some instances, He would not let the demons speak (Mark 1:23-27). In another instance, He allowed them to go into a herd of pigs (Mark 5:12,13). Yet, in all cases, Jesus was in control. He is Lord indeed! The authority He had over demons was an important mark of His Messiahship.

Jesus Delegates Authority

Jesus gave His disciples authority over demons, and they had success when they used it in His name. When Jesus' disciples returned from the mission on which He had sent them, they were joyous and excitedly reported, *"Lord, even the demons are subject to us in Your name"* (Luke 10:17). Later, when some other men, who were not true followers of Jesus, tried to copy the Apostle Paul and cast out demons, it backfired on them. They had no authority over the demons. The demons admitted they knew Jesus and

Paul, but not them. The possessed man attacked and beat them badly. When people saw this, they came to revere and magnify the name of Jesus (Acts 19:13-17).

Before Jesus ascended into heaven, He once again gave His followers authority to do His commission of preaching the Gospel to the whole world, doing miracles, and casting out demons (Mark 16:15-18). The Greek word used here for authority is *exsusia*, meaning *a delegated authority* (Matthew 28:18-20). In the Book of Acts, we can clearly see how they used the authority that Jesus delegated to them to accomplish God's purposes. Jesus said to His followers,

> *Behold, I give you the authority to trample on serpents and scorpions, and over all the power of the enemy, and nothing shall by any means hurt you* (Luke 10:19).

This authority is available for believers today, since we are partakers of His nature (2 Peter 1:4). We are in a continual spiritual warfare (Ephesians 6:10-12).We are to resist Satan (James 4:7; 1 Peter 5:8,9; Ephesians 4:7), and command evil spirits to leave people (Acts 16:18). We have the authority to do this since Jesus disarmed principalities and powers (Colossians 2:15). We are:

> *...to open their eyes and to turn them from darkness to light, and from the power of Satan to God, that they may receive forgiveness of sins and an inheritance among those who are sanctified by faith in Me* (Acts 26:18; 2 Corinthians 4:4-6).

Still today, believers take authority over evil spirits and cast out demons in Jesus' name. We are to destroy strongholds of Satan, and we do this by taking seriously the authority that is rightfully ours as followers of Jesus (2 Corinthians 10:4-6; John 1:12).

Oh, if believers only knew and exercised the authority of Jesus; if they only knew the privileges that accompany it! We have available to us all the power in the name of Jesus – the matchless name which is above every name (Philippians 2:9-11). In His name there is *salvation* (Acts 4:12), *healing* (Acts 3:6), *freedom*, and much more. When we walk in obedience to the Lord Jesus, and when His Spirit indwells us, we have His authority. With this authority and His presence, we can accomplish the purposes of God on earth.

The Apostle Paul prayed this for believers:

> *...that you may know...what is the exceeding greatness of His power toward us who believe, according to the working of His mighty power which He worked in Christ when He raised Him from the dead and seated Him at His right hand in the heavenly places, far above all principality and power and might and dominion, and every name that is named, not only in this age but also in that which is to come. And He put all things under His feet, and gave Him to be head over all things to the church, which is His body, the fullness of Him who fills all in all* (Ephesians 1:18-23; cf. Daniel 7:13,14; Revelation 15:3,4; 19:11-16).

Because of His power and authority at work within us, God is able to do much more than what we ask or think (Ephesians 3:20).

Chapter 11

The Claims of Jesus Christ

JESUS CHRIST made some marvellous claims about Himself and about His mission on earth. His claims are unique. No other person on earth could have made such claims and be believed. We know that His closest friends, and eventually His family, came to believe that what He said was true. The early church was founded on documented proof that Jesus was who He said He was. All that He did – His miracles, death, resurrection, and ascension into heaven – confirmed the truth and credibility of His claims.

Jesus' claims are very important to study and must be taken seriously, for since they came from His mouth, they must be true. Let us remember that Jesus was sinless and, therefore, could never deceive anyone (John 8:46). Let us also remember that He was the wisest Teacher and thus could not be mistaken.

Some people say that Jesus was only a prophet, a good man, or a wise teacher, but they do not believe He was the eternal Son of God. This does not make sense, for if Jesus was not who He said He was, then He would have had to be a lunatic or a liar. Then He would not have been a good man or a prophet of God, nor would He have had so many intelligent and sane people following Him and believing in Him. Throughout the centuries, and even today, many believers in Jesus have died for their faith. Most of the apostles were martyred. People just don't die for something that is false. No, Jesus' claims were all true.

I am reminded of Gamaliel's very true words, spoken to a group of people who were hostile to believers in Jesus:

> *If this plan or this work is of men, it will come to nothing; but if it is of God, you cannot overthrow it – lest you even be found to fight against God* (Acts 5:38,39).

Truly, nothing has stopped the spread of the Good News of Jesus Christ, for it is obvious that God is with His believers and is giving us the victory.

Let us consider just a few of Jesus' claims. If we were to make an in-depth study of them all, it could fill volumes.

The Claims of Jesus

1. **To be the Son of God and have a unique relationship with Him** – a relationship that no other person could have with God (John 4:34; 5:17-24; 10:30). This was evident even when He was only 12 years old. When His mother found Him at the temple, He responded, *"Did you not know that I must be about My Father's business?"* (Luke 2:49). Jesus had a self-conscious awareness, even from a young age, that He was unique, for God was His Father and He was the one and only Son.

After He began His public ministry, He expressed openly in many different ways, and in no uncertain terms, that He was God's Son. He said,

No one knows the Son except the Father. Nor does anyone know the Father except the Son, and he to whom the Son wills to reveal Him (Matthew 11:27; John 14:7).

In His words while upon the cross, He called out to God, saying, *"Abba,"* using the most intimate name that a child could use of his father. It's actually like saying, "my daddy." There is no parallel to such a term of endearment and close relationship being used of God anywhere in the Old Testament. In a clear claim of deity Jesus said, *"I and My Father are one"* (John 10:30). It was no wonder the unbelievers accused Him of blasphemy and sought for a way to kill Him.

2. **To be eternal**. Again, here is a claim of deity that He made several times. On one instance He prayed:

   And now, O Father, glorify Me together with Yourself, with the glory which I had with You before the world was (John 17:5; John 17:24; 3:31; 6:62; 8:23,58; 16:28).

   The glorified Lord Jesus claimed,

   I am the Alpha and the Omega, the Beginning and the End...who is and who was and who is to come, the Almighty (Revelation 1:8,11,17,18).

   In a very direct statement, Jesus said, *"Most assuredly, I say to you, before Abraham was, I AM"* (John 8:58).

3. **To be the I AM,** giving Himself the very personal, highest, and holiest name of God. The name that God called Himself to Moses, "*I AM*" – Ehyeh Asher Ehyeh (Exodus 3:14). Without a doubt, Jesus claimed to be God, with all the attributes, divine nature, and character of God.

   Seven times the Apostle John recorded the "*I AM*" claims of Jesus. It is significant to note that His claims are the same claims of Jehovah, the Lord God, as recorded in the Old Testament. They were claims that no ordinary person could ever dare to make. But Jesus could say them boldly since they were true, and because He ***was*** the incarnate God in human form.

   a. ***"I am the Bread of Life"*** (John 6:35; Psalm 17:15). Bread represents sustenance and life. Only God is the Life-Giver.
   b. ***"I am the Light of the World"*** (John 8:12; cf. 1:4,5; 1 John 1:5; Micah 7:8; Psalm 27:1). The Light of the World is God. He illuminates our lives.
   c. ***"I am the Door"*** (John 10:9). Jesus claimed to be the only way to God and the only way of salvation, saying, "*I am the Door. If anyone enters by Me, he will be saved*" (John 10:9). Jesus unashamedly claimed exclusivity. He is the only way to obtain salvation and only by belief in Him does one attain eternal life in heaven with God (Acts 4:12).
   d. ***"I am the Good Shepherd"*** (John 10:11). Jesus knew all the implications and ramifications of claiming to be the Good Shepherd. He gave Himself the position or role of God who is clearly portrayed in the Old Testament as being the Shepherd of His people (Ezekiel 34:15,16,23). The Psalmist sang,

"The Lord is my Shepherd" (Psalm 23:1). The people hearing Jesus would have known full well that this was a claim of deity, Messiahship, and a claim of authority and ownership over the people of God.

e. ***"I am the Resurrection and the Life"*** (John 11:25). This again is a clear claim that Jesus is God, for only God can give life (1 Samuel 2:6; John 5:25,26). Jesus proved this claim by raising people from the dead (Luke 7:14,15; 8:54,55; John 11:43,44).

f. ***"I am the Way, the Truth, and the Life"*** (John 14:6a). Jesus expanded on His divine claims by saying this. He went on to explain how He is the Way by saying, *"No one comes to the Father except through Me"* (John 14:6b). He claimed here to also be the Truth. Only God, the Perfect and Holy One, is absolute Truth. While on trial before Pilate, the Roman governor, Jesus not only claimed to be the embodiment of truth, but made yet another claim – that of being King. He explained it this way: *"You say rightly that I am a King. For this cause I was born, and for this cause I have come into the world, that I should bear witness to the truth. Everyone who is of the truth hears My voice"* (John 18:37). He also claimed that the truth would set people free (John 8:32) and that *"if the Son makes you free, you shall be free indeed"* (John 8:36; 1:17).

g. ***"I am the True Vine"*** (John 15:1,5). Jesus continued this claim by saying,

> *...you are the branches. He who abides in Me, and I in him, bears much fruit; for without Me you can do nothing* (John 15:5).

The Apostle Paul said of believers in Jesus that *"in Him we live and move and have our being"* (Acts 17:28). He is the true source of life. Without Him, we would wither and die.

Jesus is also the believer's source of peace, rest (Matthew 11:28-30), and joy. In this same context of abiding in the Vine, Jesus said, *"These things I have spoken to you, that My joy may remain in you, and that your joy may be full"* (John 15:11). Jesus loves you and wants you to be happy and have a fulfilling life of joy – a life that will be fruitful. He has told us the way to obtain this...by loving Him and keeping His commands (John 15:10,11).

4. **To have the authority to forgive sins.** Only God has this power and authority. Jesus said in public to the paralytic man who was lowered through the roof, *"Son, your sins are forgiven you"* (Mark 2:5). The critics in the crowd were thinking He was blasphemous, saying, *"Who can forgive sins but God alone?"* (Mark 2:7). Jesus, knowing their thoughts, answered them:

   "But that you may know that the Son of Man has power on earth to forgive sins." He said to the paralytic, "I say to you, arise, take up your bed..." (Mark 2:10,11).

   In another instance, Jesus told a sinful woman, *"Your sins are forgiven"* (Luke 7:48; also, He forgave another woman as recorded in John 8:11). Those who heard Him this time, however, were his friends, and they marvelled at Jesus, saying, *"Who is this who even forgives sins?"* (Luke 7:49). Their expression of awe reminds me of their words when Jesus displayed His almighty power by calming the sea: *"Who can this be? For He commands even the winds and water, and they obey Him!"* (Luke 8:25). Jesus confirmed His authority to forgive the woman's sins by telling her, *"Your faith has saved you"* (Luke 7:50). Jesus sees into the innermost heart and being of a person. Therefore, He sees their faith and their disbelief. Again, here we see Jesus' divinity, for only God can know what is in a person's heart (John 2:24,25; 13:3).

Turn your heart to Jesus, give Him the honour that is due Him (John 5:23), believe in Him and you will be saved. When you need guidance, you can rest assured that He is the Light. When you are lost, you can be confident that He is the Way. When you need healing, know that He is the Lord who heals you (Exodus 15:26; Psalm 103:3; Isaiah 53:5; Matthew 8:17; 1 Peter 2:9; Acts 9:34). When you need a friend, He will be one that sticks closer than a brother (Proverbs 18:24).

It is absolutely wrong to believe that Jesus never made these divine claims. For many different writers, at different times and at different places, all testified to their authenticity. Research has proven their writings to be authentic. If they were not true, then there would be no Christian faith and no Christian church in existence today. Therefore, with knowledge of these great claims of Jesus, each individual must have a response. Either you believe He was a lunatic or you believe the truth of His claims and confess to Jesus, as did the once doubting Thomas who said to Jesus, *"My Lord and My God"* (John 20:28).

Chapter 12

The Divine Testimony

THE TRIUNE God – Father, Son, and Holy Spirit – have testified to the truth of Jesus Christ. This is important to understand, for they have testified about who Jesus is: the eternal Son of God.

I. The Testimony of the Father (John 5:32,37; 8:18)

God testified about Jesus by His works. Jesus said,

> *...the works which the Father has given Me to finish – the very works that I do – bear witness of Me, that the Father has sent Me. And the Father Himself, who sent Me, has testified of Me* (John 5:36,37).

God testified by His divinely inspired written Word through the prophets and His own audible voice on three different occasions.

When and how did God audibly testify of Jesus?

1. **At the beginning of Jesus' ministry, at the Jordan River when Jesus was baptized** by John the Baptist, God audibly said, *"This is My beloved Son, in whom I am well pleased"* (Matthew 3:17). John said, *"I have seen and testified that this is the Son of God"* (John 1:34). Thousands of people came to John to confess their sin, repent, and be baptized (Matthew 3:5-7). However, Jesus is unique, for He was the only One who did not confess sin, since He had no sin (Matthew 3:15). God, therefore, distinguished Jesus above all others and revealed the perfection of Jesus, for He said that He was well pleased with Him. In the baptism, Jesus, the eternal Son, was seen as equal with God, the Father, and God, the Holy Spirit.

2. **In the midst of Jesus' ministry on the Mount of Transfiguration** (Matthew 17:1-9), God said, *"This is My beloved Son, in whom I am well pleased. Hear Him!"* (Matthew 17:5; cf. Luke 9:34,35). The Father testified before the disciples, thus distinguishing Jesus from His followers of the New Covenant era and also from those of the Old Covenant era, as represented on the Mount of Transfiguration by Elijah and Moses. No one is equal with Jesus, for *"He is Lord of all"* (Acts 10:36). God clearly showed Jesus' superiority when He told the disciples to listen to Jesus, for they had wanted to hear more from Elijah and Moses. Jesus is greater than any of the great men of God. Peter later recalled the transfiguration, saying, *"We...were eyewitnesses of His majesty. For He received from God the Father honour and glory"* (2 Peter 1:16-18).

3. **At the end of Jesus' ministry before He went to the cross,** the voice from heaven came in answer to Jesus' prayer that God's name would be glorified through all the coming events that Jesus was soon to endure. Jesus prayed,

   "Father, glorify Your name." Then a voice came from heaven, saying, "I have both glorified it and will glorify it again" (John 12:27,28).

   The people who heard the voice said it thundered, and all who heard knew it was supernatural. Jesus explained that the voice was heard for the sake of the listeners and that it would help to lead them to salvation in Him (John 12:30). The audible voice also served as a seal of approval on the person and work of Jesus Christ. The Father was pleased and satisfied with Jesus' obedience. Of course, God knew the outcome – that Jesus would triumph over Satan, over death, be victorious, and draw people of all nations unto Himself. Thus God's name would be glorified (John 12:31,32).

God's audible acknowledgements of Jesus testify to the truthfulness of Jesus. It validates His message and puts the divine seal upon Him. It also certifies or proves that God was satisfied, for Jesus did His will and was obedient in everything (John 4:34).

The Father sent the Son and the Father glorifies the Son, just as the Son glorifies the Father. Let us consider the unique relationship between God, the Father, and Jesus, the Son. Jesus is:

- the Son of His love (Colossians 1:13)
- the subject of His joy (Matthew 14:5; Luke 3:22)

- the brightness of His glory (Hebrews 1:3)
- the image of the invisible God (Colossians 1:15)
- the very express image of God's Person (Hebrews 1:3)
- the One who is in the bosom of His Father (John 1:18)
- known by the Father (Matthew 11:27)
- revealed by the Father (Matthew 16:16,17)
- loved by the Father (John 3:35; 5:20; John 17:24)
- honoured by the Father (John 5:23)
- the recipient of everything from the Father (John 13:3).

II. THE TESTIMONY OF JESUS ABOUT HIMSELF (John 8:13,14,18; 18:37)

Jesus' testimony about Himself is self-evident and self-explanatory. Just like a shining light is clearly evident to everyone of its existence (the light, in a sense, speaks for itself), Jesus as the Light of the World is also obvious, evident, and real. Yet there are still some people who are blind spiritually, and do not believe in Jesus. This was the case as recorded by the Apostle John. Jesus had just claimed to be the Light of the World and the Life-Giver, but His claim was challenged by the Pharisees, who said that He could not bear witness of Himself. They wanted more proof. Under their Law, there was to be at least two witnesses for a testimony to be believed as true (John 8:17). Jesus answered them, *"Even if I bear witness of Myself, My witness is true, for I know where I came from and where I am going"* (John 8:14). Jesus was the Truth and, therefore, could only speak the truth. He clearly and plainly made it known to all who He was – the unique Son of God.

Continuing to address His accusers, Jesus said, *"I am One who bears witness of Myself, and the Father who sent Me bears witness of Me"* (John 8:18). With God as His witness, He did not need two men to bear witness to the truthfulness of His words (although He has thousands, even millions of people who bear witness to Him and His truth).

At the beginning of the book of Revelation, John called Jesus, *"the faithful witness"* (Revelation 1:5). In chapter 3, we see that the eternal, glorified Jesus, the *"Alpha and the Omega,"* who is speaking to John, calls Himself, *"the Faithful and True Witness"* (Revelation 3:14). Jesus stands alone in supremacy and perfection. In this *Unique Christ* series, we have previously dealt with Jesus' testimony about Himself in the topics, *The Teachings of Jesus* and *The Miracles of Jesus* in volume one; and especially in the teaching on *The Claims of Jesus Christ* in this volume two.

The Testimony of Jesus' Works

Jesus pointed to His works as evidence of who He was. He said,

> *But I have a greater witness than John's; for the works which the Father has given Me to finish – the very works that I do – bear witness of Me, that the Father has sent Me* (John 5:36; 10:30-32,37,38; 14:9-11; 15:24; 20:30,31).

When John the Baptist questioned if Jesus was the promised Messiah, Jesus affirmed that it was true and testified that His works alone should be enough to prove it (Matthew 11:2-6). Jesus' disciples were certain that all His claims were true because they witnessed His great works on a daily basis. However, even from the very first miracle – that of changing water into wine – *"Jesus...manifested His glory; and His disciples believed in Him"* (John 2:11). Even the enemies of Jesus could not dispute His miracles, yet because of their spiritual blindness, they still would not believe in Him.

The mighty and supernatural works of Jesus revealed His divine identity (John 3:2,3), authority, character, nature, glory, grace, compassion, and love. He said, *"But if I cast out demons with the finger of God, surely the kingdom of God has come upon you"* (Luke 11:20). Jesus brought the kingdom of God to us through His presence and His works. He said, *"Believe Me that I am in the Father and the Father in Me, or else believe Me for the sake of the works themselves"* (John 14:11). As believers in Him, Jesus said that we would do supernatural works, just like Him (John 14:12-14). Let us believe it, and use the authority He has given us to do mighty works today in His name, so people will know that Jesus is Lord, and will come to experience His salvation.

III. THE TESTIMONY OF THE HOLY SPIRIT

As we have seen, the Father testified to the Son, and the Son has testified to Himself. Now let us see how the Holy Spirit testifies of Jesus. The Holy Spirit is a divine Person in the Godhead. He testified of Jesus in the past, and He continues to testify of Him today. We read in Scripture:

> *There are three who bear witness in heaven: the Father, the Word [Jesus], and the Holy Spirit; and these three are one* (1 John 5:7).

The teaching continues in the next verse to say that the Holy Spirit bears witness to Jesus on earth. The Holy Spirit is with believers today. He is our constant Comforter and

Helper. He indwells us, giving us certainty of Jesus' divinity and salvation (Romans 8:2,14,16). We read in John 15:26,

> *But when the Helper comes, whom I shall send to you from the Father, the Spirit of Truth who proceeds from the Father, He will testify of Me.*

The Holy Spirit helps us to know the truth, and thereby, know Jesus.

When Nicodemus was confused and asked Jesus about being born again, Jesus spoke in the plural on behalf of God, the Father, and God, the Holy Spirit, saying,

> *Most assuredly, I say to you, We speak what We know and testify what We have seen, and you do not receive Our witness* (John 3:11).

When you believe in Jesus, you have accepted the witness and work of the triune God (Ephesians 1:1-14).

How did the Holy Spirit testify of Jesus?

1. **At Jesus' baptism**, when He symbolically descended upon Jesus as a dove. The Holy Spirit anointed, filled, and strengthened Jesus for the task before Him, and for His mission to do the will of God and accomplish God's purposes (Luke 3:22; 4:1,14,18; Acts 10:38).

2. **Through the inspiration of the Word.** We read in God's Word that *"holy men of God spoke as they were moved by the Holy Spirit"* (2 Peter 1:21; cf. 2 Timothy 3:16; 1 Peter 1:10,11). It was the inspiration of the Holy Spirit that caused them to prophesy about Jesus. The Holy Spirit also inspired the New Testament writers to testify about Jesus, for He is the Spirit of Truth (John 16:13; 1 John 5:6).

3. **Through the empowerment of gifts.** We read in the letter to the Hebrews that the salvation of Jesus is confirmed by *"God also bearing witness both with signs and wonders, with various miracles, and gifts of the Holy Spirit, according to His own will"* (Hebrews 2:4). The power of the Holy Spirit was vital to the growth of the early church, as it still is today. Jesus instructed His followers to wait until the Holy Spirit had come upon them. Then they were to go out and fulfill His Great Commission. They did just this:

   They went out and preached everywhere, the Lord working with them and confirming the word through the accompanying signs (Mark 16:20).

   The Holy Spirit's gift of speaking in other tongues testifies to Jesus. On the Day of Pentecost, when the Holy Spirit descended upon the believers who were assembled in the Upper Room, they began to speak in various other languages; in tongues that were not known to them. The gift of tongues can be both languages of men and of angels (1 Corinthians 13:1), the latter being a heavenly language which is unknown upon the earth. The tongues of men are known languages, yet unknown to the one speaking it. Many people from other countries and languages heard them speaking as they were moved by the Holy Spirit. They said, *"We hear them speaking in our own tongues the wonderful works of God"* (Acts 2:11). They heard of the glorious salvation of Jesus that the Holy Spirit was declaring! The response was great and over 3,000 people became believers in Jesus on that day! (Acts 2:41).

4. **The Holy Spirit testified of Jesus through the disciples** who boldly witnessed with His power. Jesus had promised the coming of the Holy Spirit. He said, *"But you shall receive power when the Holy Spirit has come upon you; and you shall be witnesses to Me"* (Acts 1:8). It did, in fact, happen just as Jesus said. Soon after their supernatural experience in the Upper Room on the Day of Pentecost, the apostles affirmed,

   And we are His witnesses to these things, and so also is the Holy Spirit whom God has given to those who obey Him (Acts 5:32).

   The Holy Spirit is pleased to fill every believer, that we might be a bold witness for Jesus. Paul was filled with the Spirit (Acts 9:17) and empowered to do a mighty work for God. He claimed,

   ...in mighty signs and wonders, by the power of the Spirit of God...I have fully preached the gospel of Christ (Romans 15:19; 1 Corinthians 2:4,5; 1 Thessalonians 1:5).

   The Apostle Paul taught, saying,

   Therefore I make known to you that no one speaking by the Spirit of God calls Jesus accursed, and no one can say that Jesus is Lord except by the Holy Spirit (1 Corinthians 12:3).

Would you say these words out loud right now? "Jesus is Lord!" Hallelujah!

Chapter 13

The Old Covenant Testimony of Jesus

LET US first consider the testimony of the most prominent person in the Old Covenant – that of Moses.

I. The Testimony of Moses (John 5:45-47)

Moses was one of the greatest witnesses of Jesus Christ, both in his person and through his writings. He prophesied about the Lord and clearly spoke of Him (Genesis 3:15; 12:3; 49:10, cf. Galatians 4:4):

> *And the Lord said to me: "...I will raise up for them a Prophet like you from among their brethren, and will put My words in His mouth, and He shall speak to them all that I command Him. And it shall be that whoever will not hear My words which He speaks in My name, I will require it of him"* (Deuteronomy 18:17-19; John 4:25; Acts 3:22,23).

Clearly, the Lord Jesus Christ was the Prophet who was

foretold. The Lord said that the Prophet He would raise up would be one like Moses.

How was Jesus a Prophet like Moses?

1. **They both did great miracles.** Moses was the first who did great and mighty miracles of God; Jesus, however, did greater miracles of God.

2. **They both served as prophet, priest, and king.** Moses is the only one, other than Jesus, who served in the three different offices of prophet (Deuteronomy 34:10), priest (Deuteronomy 33:4,5), and king (Psalm 99:6). Jesus, however, is a greater Prophet, for on the Mount of Transfiguration, in the presence of Moses, God directed the attention toward Jesus and told the disciples, *"Hear Him!"* (Matthew 17:5). Moses was a great leader acting as a king over the people, but Jesus is the King of kings! Moses was a priest, but Jesus is the Great High Priest, according to the order of Melchizedek – the divine order of the King of Righteousness, which is what the name Melchizedek means (Hebrews 7:1,21).

3. **They were both mediators of God's covenant with humankind.** Moses was a mediator of the Old Covenant, the Law (John 1:17), but Jesus is the Mediator of a new and better covenant (Hebrews 7:22; 9:15).

4. **They both spoke the word of God.** Jesus not only spoke the word, but He is the living Word of God (John 1:1; Hebrews 1:1-4).

5. **They both sacrificed to God.** Moses offered animal sacrifices, but Jesus offered Himself, the Perfect Sacrifice – the Lamb of God (Hebrews 9:12-14).

6. **They were both used by God to bring salvation and deliverance.** Moses was the instrument that God used to save and deliver the nation of Israel from bondage in Egypt; Jesus Himself saves and delivers all who believe in Him from the bondage of sin.

7. **They both exposed sin.** Moses accused the people of sin, like a prosecutor (John 5:45,46; 7:19); but Jesus atoned for our sin, made intercession, and has become our Advocate (Isaiah 53:12; Luke 23:34).

In each similarity noted, there are important differences which show the superiority and supremacy of Jesus. For example, Moses could not see the face of God (Exodus 33:20), but Jesus saw the Father and was His exact image (John 1:18; Hebrews 1:3). The Law was given by Moses, but grace and truth came through Jesus (James 1:17). The writer to the Hebrews also makes a distinction in position by saying, *"Moses indeed was faithful in all His house as a servant...but Christ as a Son over His own house"* (Hebrews 3:5). Moses endured hardship because he understood that the reward he would attain from Christ for faithfulness was far greater than the riches of Egypt (Hebrews 11:26,27). Moses' desire has been fulfilled, for in heaven *"they sing the song of Moses, the servant of God, and the song of the Lamb"* (Revelation 15:3).

Moses and the other prophets of old rejoiced at the time of salvation brought by Jesus (1 Peter 1:9,10). Jesus was what they had all longed for and He was the object of their hope (Acts 10:42,43). Truly, our only hope is in Him (Colossians 1:27).

II. THE TESTIMONY OF JOHN THE BAPTIST

Now, although John the Baptist was written of in the books of the New Covenant, he actually belonged to the Old Covenant time, for he lived, ministered, and died before the completion of the New Covenant when Jesus accomplished redemption on the cross. John was considered by people to be a great prophet and a great man of God. He had much influence in his day, and surprisingly, even today he has followers in Iraq. He was a man of principle, with the highest moral character, integrity, purity, and humility. Jesus said that John was truly the greatest man of the Old Testament age, or the age of the Law (Matthew 11:11). All the other prophets spoke about the coming of the Messiah, but John is the only one who had the privilege of announcing that the Messiah had arrived. He also had the task of preparing the way for the Lord Jesus. John served as a bridge between the period of Law and the period of grace through the New Covenant of our Lord Jesus (Matthew 11:8-11).

Jesus Himself affirmed that John the Baptist's witness of Him was true when He said, *"You have sent to John, and he has borne witness to the truth"* (John 5:32,33).

How did John the Baptist witness of Jesus? He attested:

1. **That Jesus was the promised Messiah.** When John was asked if he was the Christ, he said no, another was coming. When Jesus came, John then announced, *"This is He of whom I said, 'After me comes a Man who is preferred before me'"* (John 1:30).

2. **To the redemptive power of Jesus.** He said of Him, *"Behold! The Lamb of God who takes away the sin of the world!"* (John 1:29; John 3:36).

3. **That Jesus was eternal.** Even though John was a few months older than Jesus, he said, "*He was before me*" (John 1:30).

4. **To the deity of Jesus.** He called Him, "*Son of God*" (John 1:34), and said that He "*comes from above*" (John 3:31).

5. **To the work of Jesus,** saying He was anointed with the Spirit of God who descended and remained upon Him. John also said of Jesus, "*This is He who baptizes with the Holy Spirit*" (John 1:33; cf. Matthew 3:11).

6. **That Jesus is the Great Judge,** saying, "*His winnowing fan is in His hand, and He will thoroughly purge His threshing floor, and gather His wheat into the barn; but He will burn up the chaff with unquenchable fire*" (Matthew 3:12).

7. **That Jesus gives everlasting life.** John said, "*He who believes in the Son has everlasting life; and he who does not believe the Son shall not see life, but the wrath of God abides on him*" (John 3:36).

8. **That Jesus was sent from God and spoke the words of God,** saying, "*For He whom God has sent speaks the words of God*" (John 3:34).

9. **To the superiority of Jesus,** saying, "*He...is preferred before me, whose sandal strap I am not worthy to loose*" (John 1:27,30; cf. Matthew 3:11). John also said to Jesus, "*I have need to be baptized by you...*" (Matthew 3:14).

10. **To the nature of Christ** as the true Light (John 1:7-9).

How is Jesus superior to John or to any other prophet?

- **position** – He is from heaven (John 3:31)
- **Sonship** – having a unique and special relationship with God (John 3:35)
- **in His teaching** (John 3:32-34).

The witness of John the Baptist testifies to the truth of Jesus' divine calling, anointing, mission, and purpose. John's witness also proves the superiority of Jesus and His deity, and that He has the names, character, glory, and works of God. John's witness proves that Jesus fits the criteria of being God, for he said that if you believe in Jesus, you will, likewise, certify that God is true (John 3:33).

III. THE TESTIMONY OF THE HOLY BOOKS

Jesus clearly stated repeatedly that Scripture wrote about Him. Of course, the Scripture He was referring to was the Old Testament. He said,

> *All things must be fulfilled which were written in the Law of Moses and the Prophets and the Psalms concerning Me* (Luke 24:44).

When Jesus began His public ministry, He declared in the synagogue in Nazareth that the portion of Scripture He read from the Prophet Isaiah about the Messiah's ministry, was that day fulfilled by Him. The people in the synagogue did not believe Jesus and were so angry that they wanted to kill Him. To these same type of self-righteous people, Jesus later responded:

> *You search the Scriptures, for in them you think you have eternal life; and these are they which testify of*

> *me.... For if you believed Moses, you would believe Me; for he wrote about Me* (John 5:39,46).

Jesus exposed their blindness to the truth, for even though they thought they were on the right path – the path to eternal life – they were not. It is only by belief in Jesus that one obtains eternal life. He said, *"The words that I speak to you are spirit, and they are life"* (John 6:63). Jesus spoke the truth, for He was the truth. He also said, *"You shall know the truth, and the truth shall make you free"* (John 8:32). The people who did not believe in Jesus were spiritually blind. As the Apostle Paul explained,

> *But the natural man does not receive the things of the Spirit of God, for they are foolishness to him; nor can he know them, because they are spiritually discerned* (1 Corinthians 2:14).

Paul prayed that...

> *...the Father of glory, may give to you the spirit of wisdom and revelation in the knowledge of Him, the eyes of your understanding being enlightened...* (Ephesians 1:17,18; Psalm 119:130).

I pray this same prayer for you that God may enlighten you to see the truth in Jesus Christ.

The risen Lord Jesus appeared on the road to Emmaus to enlighten His two doubting disciples. He said, "*O foolish ones, and slow of heart to believe in all that the prophets have spoken!*" (Luke 24:25), and then He opened up the Scripture to them. Luke explains that...

> *...beginning at Moses and all the Prophets, He expounded to them in all the Scriptures the things concerning Himself* (Luke 24:27).

Later that same day in Jerusalem, Jesus did the same for all 11 disciples (Luke 24:44,45). He wanted them to be sure they understood clearly two things in particular, for these things comprise the foundation of our faith:

- Scripture was about Him and He fulfilled it.
- He is alive and alive forevermore. Certainly Jesus accomplished this, for all their doubts were gone.

The Apostles affirmed that Old Testament Scripture testified about Jesus

The Apostle Paul declared that he preached about Jesus *"according to the Scriptures"* (1 Corinthians 15:3,4). Jesus is clearly portrayed throughout the whole Old Testament. He was actively involved in His person, and there are numerous prophecies about Him. He is symbolized and typified in every temple ritual and in every animal sacrifice.

The Apostle Peter confirmed in his letters that the prophets prophesied of Jesus' salvation of grace, His sufferings, and His glories (1 Peter 1:9-12,23-25). Peter explained that the prophecies were given by God's will and by the Holy Spirit (2 Peter 1:20,21). The Old Testament served to shed a light which was intended to point us to Christ. Peter declared,

> *We also have the prophetic word made more sure, which you do well to heed as a light that shines in a dark place, until the day dawns and the morning star rises in your hearts* (2 Peter 1:19).

If a person sincerely seeks after God and wants the truth, Jesus will always be revealed (Matthew 11:27).

The word of God, in both the Old and New Testaments, are important for the believer in Jesus (2 Timothy 3:16,17).

Some Christians neglect the Old Testament, but I urge you not to, for as we have seen, the Old Testament testifies about Jesus. When you read the Old Testament with faith in Jesus Christ, a new light is shed on its meaning and significance.

Chapter 14

THE NEW COVENANT TESTIMONY OF JESUS

WE HAVE looked at many different testimonies of Jesus: the divine testimony of the triune God, and the Old Covenant testimony of Jesus. Now let us delve into the New Covenant testimony of Jesus, which includes the testimony of the apostles and other disciples of Jesus.

I. THE TESTIMONY OF THE APOSTLES

First, let us consider the testimony of Jesus' disciples. They had lived with Him for over three years. They were His friends and His students. They saw His perfect life. They heard His glorious teachings, witnessed all the undisputed miracles, saw His crucifixion (John 19:34,35), and more importantly, witnessed Him alive from the dead – all which gave their testimony of His credibility and authority.

Their testimony is twofold, being comprised of not only historical knowledge, but also spiritual knowledge. After personally experiencing the infilling of the Holy Spirit, they had a new dimension or a new enlightenment of spiritual things (Acts 2:1-4; 5:32). They were radically transformed from the inside out. God had given them new boldness and new spiritual insight so they could successfully carry out Jesus' Great Commission and teach others about Him (Luke 24:46-49; Acts 1:8; 20:24; 26:16-18). Their writings, as we read today in the New Testament, verify the truth of Jesus and help us to understand spiritual truths. They were committed to preaching about Jesus Christ in a hostile environment, and most were martyred for what they knew to be true.

What truths about Jesus did the disciples proclaim?

1. **Nathanael, from Cana, also known as Bartholomew,** proclaimed to Jesus, *"You are the Son of God! You are the King of Israel!"* (John 1:49). His words were true. Remember that Jesus had said of Nathanael, *"Behold, an Israelite indeed, in whom is no guile!"* (John 1:47).

2. **Thomas** declared to Jesus after being convinced of His resurrection, *"My Lord and my God!"* (John 20:28).

3. **Peter** confessed, *"You are the Christ, the Son of the living God"* (Matthew 16:16). On another occasion, Peter spoke for himself and the other disciples, saying: *"We have come to believe and know that You are the Christ, the Son of the living God"* (John 6:69). He also claimed,

   > *We did not follow cunningly devised fables when we made known to you the power and coming of our Lord Jesus Christ, but were eyewitnesses of His majesty* (2 Peter 1:16; cf. Acts 2:32; 3:15; 4:13,20).

In his sermon on the day of Pentecost, Peter claimed that Jesus proved He was the Messiah by all the miracles He did. He affirmed that Jesus was crucified and died on the cross (Acts 2:22,23). On another occasion, when Peter healed the man who had been born lame, he told the amazed onlookers that it was done through the power of the name of Jesus, the same holy and just One they had killed, but whom God had raised from the dead. Peter told the crowd that these facts were confirmed by many eyewitnesses (Acts 3:12-15). He also witnessed about Jesus' deity, perfection (1 Peter 2:22), salvation, and Second Coming (1 Peter 2:24; 2 Peter 3:8-13).

4. **Matthew** wrote his Gospel account to prove to the Jews that Jesus was the King and the Messiah, the Son of David, and that the prophecies were fulfilled in Him.

5. **Philip** declared to have found the Messiah (John 1:45).

6. **James** witnessed unceasingly about Jesus at the cost of his life, being the first of the apostles to be martyred (Acts 12:1,2).

7. **John** declared his testimony to be true (John 21:24) and wrote the reason for his Gospel account:

   These are written that you may believe that Jesus is the Christ, the Son of God, and that believing you may have life in His name (John 20:31; John 1:14; 1 John 4:14; Revelation 1:2).

   John stressed that his witness and the witness of the other apostles about Jesus is true and certain, saying, "*We have heard...we have seen with our eyes...our hands have handled"* (1 John 1:1-3). John asserted, *"This is the message which we have heard from Him"* (1 John 1:5).

The Testimony of the Apostle Paul

Now, to be considered an apostle, the person had to have been chosen by Jesus and witnessed His teaching, preaching, and supernatural ministry while He was on the earth. The apostle must also have been an eyewitness of the risen Lord Jesus (Acts 1:21,22).

Saul of Tarsus, who came to be known as the Apostle Paul, is considered an apostle, because the risen Lord Jesus appeared to him and chose him (Acts 9; 22:7-10,15; 26:16-18; 1 Corinthians 15:8-10). Saul was a resident of Jerusalem. Could it be that he witnessed some of the teaching, preaching, and miracles of Jesus? Is it possible that he was among the group of Pharisees that Jesus rebuked? Did the death of Stephen (the first Christian martyr) that Saul witnessed, have an impact on him? (Acts 7:58-60; 22:20).

A seed must have been planted deep within Saul's heart, for he readily came to believe after Jesus appeared to him. Paul declared that he preached about Jesus *"according to the Scriptures"* (1 Corinthians 15:3,4), and he knew the Scriptures well since he had been a well-trained religious Pharisee. Not only Paul's words, but the radical change in his life, proved that the living Lord Jesus was real to him and near to him. Paul testified about Jesus: *"In Him dwells all the fullness of the Godhead bodily"* (Colossians 2:9). Paul had the gift of teaching great spiritual truths, which he accredited to the revelation of the Holy Spirit, for he had been filled with the Holy Spirit (1 Corinthians 2:6-16).

As we know, the early church had the Old Testament Scriptures, but they also had the words of Jesus that were memorized and recorded by the eyewitnesses, the apostles. These early recordings were, like the Old Testament, inspired by the Holy Spirit of God, and came to be circulated among the churches. Eventually, they were compiled as a complete canon of Holy Scripture about the New Covenant of God through Jesus Christ. The Apostle Paul exhorted the first century church of Colosse:

> *Let the word of Christ dwell in you richly in all wisdom, teaching and admonishing one another in psalms and hymns and spiritual songs...* (Colossians 3:16).

Thank God for the faithful witness of the apostles. God used them in a great way, and as a result, we have a true and accurate record of Jesus Christ today.

II. The Testimony of Other Disciples

Let us also consider the testimony of other disciples whose lives were changed by Jesus. They testified to the deity and Lordship of Jesus Christ. In fact, everyone who met Him was somehow changed. The writer to the Hebrews reports that there was a great cloud of witnesses who could testify to all that Jesus endured and also testify to His triumph (Hebrews 12:1,2).

In the Bible, we read of:

1. **Nicodemus,** who said, "*Rabbi, we know that You are a teacher come from God; for no one can do these signs that You do unless God is with him*" (John 3:2).
2. **The Samaritan woman and many people of her town** confessed: "*We have heard for ourselves and know that this is indeed the Christ, the Saviour of the world*" (John 4:42; 4:29).

3. **Martha,** the sister of Lazarus whom Jesus raised from the dead, confessed to believe that Jesus was the promised Messiah, the Son of God (John 11:27).

4. **The demoniac** who had been delivered by Jesus became a witness for Him (Mark 5:20).

5. **Zacchaeus'** salvation and that of his household (Luke 19:1-10).

6. **Mary Magdalene,** from whom Jesus cast out seven demons (John 20:11-18), and many other followers, were living proof of the miraculous power of Jesus.

Other testimonies of Jesus came from unexpected and surprising sources:

7. **Even demons** testify that Jesus is the Son of God (Mark 1:23,24; 5:6,7; Luke 4:41; Acts 19:15).

8. **Judas** confessed to have betrayed innocent blood (Matthew 27:4).

9. **The high priest Caiaphas,** without realizing the significance, said that Jesus would die for the nation (John 11:47-52).

10. **Pilate and his wife** were upset by the people's hostility toward a man they knew to be faultless and just (Matthew 27:19-25). Tradition holds that Pilate's wife became a believer in Jesus.

11. **The thief on the cross** beside Jesus confessed that Jesus had done nothing wrong, and asked Jesus to remember him when He came into His kingdom (Luke 23:41,42).

12. **The centurion** who crucified Jesus, confessed, *"Truly this Man was the Son of God!"* (Mark 15:39; Matthew 27:54).

13. **The angels** proclaimed the deity of Jesus (Luke 1:32,35), His eternal kingdom (Luke 1:31-33), His salvation for humankind (Matthew 1:20-23), His perfection (as in Luke 1:35, when He was called by the divine name of "Holy One"), and that He was the Messiah (Luke 2:11) who would bring great joy (Luke 2:10).

Even today and throughout past generations, people's lives have been changed by the living Lord Jesus. When you put your faith in Him, you are a changed person. You are made new. Jesus is real. Jesus is who He claimed to be: the divine Son of God. I know this from my own personal experience. When I came to believe in Jesus, He saved me from sin and gave me eternal life. Only God could do that! Believe in Him today and you, too, will be saved. If Jesus has touched your life, I pray that you will be a genuine witness to proclaim Him, to lead people to the truth; and through the word of your testimony, Satan will be defeated (Revelation 12:11; Acts 20:24; 26:16-18; Matthew 24:14).

Chapter 15

The Teaching of Jesus on Heaven and Rewards

EVERY BELIEVER in Jesus, who has been made righteous through Him, is given the greatest possible reward – that of eternal life and the bliss of forever being in the presence of the Lord. Jesus said to His disciples,

> *And if I go and prepare a place for you, I will come again and receive you to Myself; that where I am, there you may be also* (John 14:3).

Jesus claimed:

> *I am the resurrection and the life. He who believes in Me, though he may die, he shall live. And whoever lives and believes in Me shall never die...* (John 11:25,26).

The gracious gift of eternal life is a present reality, as well as a future promise (John 3:36; 1 Timothy 4:8). What a joyous existence that will be! It will certainly not be boring or spent strumming a harp on a cloud, as some comics or cartoons depict. Rather it will be a life of joyous and active service and worship to God.

When Jesus taught His Jewish listeners, He did not have to tell them that there was an afterlife. They already believed in that. But He did correct them when they were mistaken about the nature of the heavenly existence. For example, thinking that a man would have a wife in heaven implies a sexual relationship. Jesus corrected them by saying that there would be no marriage in heaven, for the resurrected body would not be as our body is now, which is suited to earth and has natural desires. No, the resurrected body will be one suited to heaven. There will be no sexuality in heaven but, rather, as Jesus said, we will be like the angels (Matthew 22:29-32). The people who questioned Jesus had the wrong idea of heaven, as do some people today, thinking that heaven will be a place of sensual or physical rewards. This is absurd! How could life in heaven be at all related to our frail, physical bodies, lusts, or appetites. Our heavenly desire will be for God alone and to serve and worship Him, not to serve our own appetites or pleasures, for that would be unthinkable in heaven!

It is within the consciousness of humankind to believe in life after death. Both the Old and New Testaments shed much light on the afterlife. Scripture teaches that the believer in Jesus, after he or she dies, will be resurrected to life – a new life in the spiritual realm. It will not only be endless life, but it will be life in all its fullness (Matthew 25:46). We will have new interests and new jobs. Our joy will be complete, since the reason for our creation and existence will be fully realized. We will be restored to the closeness with God that Adam enjoyed in the garden before the Fall, when sin entered the world.

Heaven is described in Scripture by various names:

1. **Paradise**, or literally, *"a garden,"* which conveys the idea of a place of great beauty (Revelation 2:7; 2 Corinthians 12:2-4). Jesus told the repentant and believing thief who was on the cross beside Him that he would be with Him in Paradise (Luke 23:43).

2. **His Father's house** with many mansions which conveys the thoughts of rest, safety, and a home (John 14:2).

3. **Heavenly country** conveys the thoughts of a homeland, a place of citizenship for those in the kingdom of God (Hebrews 11:13-16; Philippians 3:20,21).

4. **City** means that heaven is an organized society with much activity (Hebrews 11:10; Revelation 21:2).

What are the blessings of heaven?

1. **Continual fellowship with Jesus Christ** (John 14:3; 2 Corinthians 5:1,8; Philippians 1:23; Revelation 21:3; 22:4). We shall see His face, for as Jesus said, *"Blessed are the pure in heart for they shall see God"* (Matthew 5:8). The redeemed will see God in the face of the Lord Jesus Christ.

2. **Fullness of knowledge** – the most important knowledge being the knowledge of God (1 Corinthians 13:12).

3. **Rest and ultimate peace.** There will be no sin, curse, pain, nor sorrow (Revelation 14:13; 21:4).

4. **Service to God** (Revelation 7:15; 22:3).
5. **Joy**, for there will be no tears (Revelation 21:4).
6. **Permanence and stability**, for the happiness of heaven will last forever.
7. **Social interaction**, since we will be in the company of angels and gathered together with others who have been redeemed (Hebrews 12:22,23; 1 Thessalonians 4:17).
8. **Light and beauty**. The light, which is unceasing, is like none other we have seen before. The beauty of heaven is hard for our limited minds to comprehend, for nothing on earth can compare to it (Revelation 21:23; 22:5).

Divine Judgement

Just as the idea of an afterlife is a part of man's conscience, so is the notion of a divine judgement. God is the Judge of all, and He performs this work through Jesus Christ to whom He has given all judgement (John 5:22,23; Hebrews 12:23). Scripture teaches that there will be several judgements, and one is the judgement of the righteous that will take place when Jesus Christ returns (Matthew 16:27; Revelation 22:12). Here the Lord will judge the works of the believers and bestow rewards (Romans 14:10-12; 2 Corinthians 5:10; 1 Corinthians 3:11-15; 4:5).

It will not be a judgement for sin, since the Lord atoned our sins upon the cross and removed them (Romans 8:1). We know from Scripture that the wages of sin is death (Romans 6:23), but death cannot keep us. For although our bodies will die, we will live forever. Jesus said,

> *Most assuredly, I say to you, he who hears My word and believes in Him who sent Me has everlasting life, and shall not come into judgement, but has passed from death into life* (John 5:24).

In several of Jesus' parables, He taught about this judgement, such as in the parable of the talents (Matthew 25:14-30), and the parables of the ten minas or pounds (Luke 19:11-27), and the parable of the labourers (Matthew 20:1-16). Every believer will be called to give an account of the use he or she has made of their talents, money, responsibilities, and the opportunities that God has entrusted to them. The works that are tried by fire and remain will be rewarded (1 Corinthians 3:13,14).

The Apostle Paul states that salvation is a gift of God, given by grace:

> *...not of works, lest anyone should boast. For we are His workmanship, created in Christ Jesus for good works which God prepared beforehand that we should walk in them* (Ephesians 2:9,10).

In other words, God has given us opportunities to do as Jesus told us: *"Lay up for yourself treasures in heaven"* (Matthew 6:20).

What will lead to a heavenly reward?

1. **Leading others to know the Lord** is the most important thing we can do as believers – and this will be rewarded (Daniel 12:3; Proverbs 11:30; 1 Thessalonians 2:19,20; James 5:20). Jesus made it clear that labour in His harvest field will reap a reward (John 4:36).

2. **Being a faithful steward** of all God has entrusted to us, like Jesus' parables taught (Matthew 20:1; 25:14; Luke 19:11; 1 Corinthians 4:1-5; Galatians 6:7-10).

3. **Doing good to all men,** especially to fellow believers who are in need (Galatians 6:10; 2 Peter 1:7). Jesus taught that hospitality is rewarded (Matthew 10:40,41), and so is caring for the sick, the poor and the persecuted (Matthew 25:34-40). Even giving a cup of cold water to one in need will be rewarded (Matthew 10:42). Doing good means having Christ-like virtues which include brotherly kindness and love – all which ensure that...

   ...an entrance will be supplied to you abundantly into the everlasting kingdom of our Lord and Saviour Jesus Christ (2 Peter 1:11).

   God will reward the labour of love (Hebrews 6:10; 1 Corinthians 15:58).

4. **Enduring suffering** and remaining true to the Lord Jesus in an evil world (Matthew 5:11,12; Luke 6:22,23; 2 Timothy 2:12; James 1:12).

5. **Self-sacrifice.** Jesus said that everyone who has sacrificed *"for My name's sake, shall receive a hundredfold, and inherit everlasting life"* (Matthew19:29).

The nature of the reward is represented by the figure of the crown; an *"imperishable crown"* as Paul describes it (1 Corinthians 9:25). Souls won to the Lord are our *"crown of rejoicing"* (1 Thessalonians 2:19). In other Scripture, the reward is called a *"crown of righteousness"* (2 Timothy 4:8), *"the crown of life"* (James 1:12; Revelation 2:10), and the *"crown of glory"* (1 Peter 5:4). In some way this crown is a mark of distinction that shows the Lord's pleasure bestowed upon the one to whom it was given.

Let us read of a final reward that Jesus spoke of: *"To him who overcomes I will grant to sit with Me on My throne"* (Revelation 3:21). This means we will reign with Him forever (2 Timothy 2:11,12). We, who are in Christ, have a glorious hope of glory! (Colossians 1:27).

Chapter 16

The Teaching of Jesus on Violence

OUR LORD Jesus Christ was a man of peace. He taught and exemplified it. One of His titles is the Prince of Peace. He stood with the oppressed and defended the victims of violence. For example, the woman caught in adultery would have been stoned had it not been for Jesus (John 8:3). Obviously, He was a champion of human rights and social justice. His defence, however, never entailed violence.

In the Garden of Gethsemane, when the enemies of Jesus came to arrest Him, one of His followers cut off a man's ear with a sword (John 18:10). Jesus rebuked His misguided follower and upheld peace and non-violence by saying, *"Put your sword in its place, for all who take the sword will perish by the sword"* (Matthew 26:52). Jesus proved that violence was not the way. He responded to the violence of His enemies with compassion, even healing the man whose ear had been severed (Luke 22:50,51). He spoke calmly and cooperated with them, although He knew their intention was to cause Him to suffer a violent death. He could have called on a host of angels to prevent it. Instead, He permitted the events to happen because He loves all people and willingly sacrificed His own life to give life, freedom, and salvation to those who would believe in Him. In so doing, Jesus fulfilled the plan of God for redemption, as well as fulfilling all the prophecies spoken of Him.

In another example from the life of Jesus, He taught us not to retaliate or take revenge – that is the Lord's prerogative alone (Romans 12:17-21). When people rejected Jesus in Samaria, John and James wanted Him to call down fire to destroy them, but Jesus rebuked His beloved followers (Luke 9:51-56). This was not His way, nor was it consistent with His Spirit.

What are some reasons for non-violence?

1. **We are to follow Jesus' example** (1 Peter 2:21-23). Christian ethics – the way we are to live as taught by Jesus – is the supreme and ultimate code of behaviour (Matthew 5:48).

2. **Violence breeds more violence.** Jesus warned, "*...all who take the sword will perish by the sword*" (cf. 1 Thessalonians 5:15). History has proven this to be true. To respond with violence resolves nothing but promotes hatred and more acts of violence. In addition to the victims, it is also hurtful for the perpetrator. If we followed "*an eye for an eye and a tooth for a tooth*" (Matthew 5:38), it wouldn't be long before everyone was blind and toothless. In Jesus' great and radical Sermon on the Mount, He taught us to turn the other cheek (Matthew 5:39). He said,

*Love your enemies, bless those who curse you, do good to those who hate you, and pray for those who spitefully use you and persecute you (*Matthew 5:44).

3. **Violence is against the will of God,** and is not an option. God created humankind in His image (Genesis 9:5,6). Therefore, every person is of utmost importance and worthy of respect. No one has the right to spill another person's blood. Only God has the right to take life. Since the fall of humankind into sin, violence has been a constant problem. Very early in human history, Cain killed his brother Abel. He resorted to violence, and God punished him (Genesis 4:8-15). Jesus tells us about the violent end to some Galileans and to others near Jerusalem who were crushed when a tower fell on them. God allowed it to happen, for Jesus warned that unless every person repents, a violent punishment awaits them (Luke 13:1-5). There will be a judgement day, and we must all give an account when we stand before God.

4. **Violence brings a curse** (Deuteronomy 28:24,25). Countries have been cursed and punished by God for sin and violence. In the Old Testament, God used the children of Israel as instruments to punish the Canaanites for sin and violence that had reached the limit (Genesis 15:16).

5. **Non-violence brings a reward.** In Scripture, we read that if you show kindness to an enemy, the Lord will reward you (Proverbs 25:21,22; Romans 13:1-4).

6. **We are to obey the laws of the land.** We must respect human authority. Laws are made to bring peace to individuals, to communities, and to the country. Justice and truth must be served for those who commit violent acts.

The Christian's Purpose

How, then, should the Christian respond to acts of violence or acts of terrorism? We truly mourn with the families of those who died on September 11th, 2001, and all other victims of terrorism, and we keep them in our prayers. All acts of terrorism and other types of violence have their roots in sin. Satan roams about seeking whom He may devour (1 Peter 5:8; John 10:10). I believe it is a demonic influence that causes people to become suicide bombers. As followers of Christ, we must be careful not to generalize or be prejudiced. Terrorists are a small fanatical minority. Most people want to live with their neighbours in peace.

We are engaged in a spiritual warfare. The Apostle Paul exhorted:

> *Put on the whole armour of God, that you may be able to stand against the wiles of the devil. For we do not wrestle against flesh and blood* (Ephesians 6:11,12).

In this same passage, it is interesting that the righteous soldier moves about *"with the preparation of the gospel of peace"* (Ephesians 6:15). Jesus gave the church a task – to bring the Gospel message wherever we go. Our Christian response to terrorism must be one of love, compassion, and a determination to share the love of Jesus with those who are blind to the truth. The greatest power and strength that a person can have is to love and forgive. For example, Stephen, the first Christian martyr, forgave his killers and influenced Paul.

The example of our Lord Jesus is perfect and wonderful, but sadly, many who call themselves "Christians" have been bad examples and have committed terrible acts of violence. Sometimes these were done in the name of Jesus Christ, such as the church-sanctioned crusades from the 11th to the 13th century, the Spanish Inquisition, and more recently, the Salem witch trials in America – all which surely grieved our Lord. Christians have even killed other Christians. All these evil actions are not in keeping with the Christian faith. They were carried out by people who did not model Christ – as every true Christian should. In many cases, the people involved in the violence were only "Christian" *by name* and not *by heart*. Many of them never read a Bible for themselves. They were ignorant of the truth and not truly converted; never having experienced the transforming power of Jesus Christ; never becoming citizens of heaven (John 18:36).

From history we see that whenever people became true followers of Jesus Christ, good and peaceful things came about. True Christians have built schools, hospitals, orphanages, homeless shelters, and relief organizations such as The Red Cross and World Vision. Christianity has had the greatest influence for good in the world. Godly men, such as John Wesley in the early 1700s, started a mass protest against slavery. It was believing Christian people who were ultimately responsible for the abolition of slavery. In South Africa, followers of Christ paved the way for peace and brought an end to years of violence.

The only hope for peace in this world is in Jesus Christ. In preparation for His crucifixion and ascension into heaven, Jesus said to His followers, *"Peace I leave with you, My peace I give to you; not as the world gives do I give to you"* (John 14:27).

To be like Jesus is to have a loving tolerance toward people of other beliefs, but to also witness to them about the truth, pray for them, peacefully oppose violence and injustice, and be a Christ-like model. Yes, Jesus was peaceful, but that did not mean He was weak or passive (John 18:22,23). He did everything with a divine agenda and purpose. He was fearless and spoke harshly and forcefully against the wickedness of the self-righteous Pharisees. When He cleared the temple of the corrupt merchants and overturned their tables, it was a violent display against sin, not violence against the persons involved.

I am reminded of Jesus' parable of the wheat and the tares. No violence was permitted against the tares. Only God can truly judge people's hearts, for we are not qualified to judge others (Matthew 7:1). On Judgement Day, the Lord will take the tares and burn them, but the good wheat – the righteous sons of the kingdom – will remain and shine for God (Matthew 13:24-30; 36-43; Philippians 2:15).

Jesus brings personal peace to the individual who submits and believes in Him. In turn, peace is shown by the believer to all with whom he comes in contact. The true believer is a strong proponent of peace in the world, and prays for peace.

We know that prayer changes things, so I encourage every believer to daily pray for peace in this world. The war and turmoil in the Middle East, where I come from, is distressing. There are many injustices, but very few stand on the side of the oppressed. Many people say they want peace, but these are empty words, since their actions are not peaceful. There will never be peace among the ungodly, for only in Jesus Christ does humankind find peace, and keep it.

Chapter 17

The Names and Titles of Jesus

The names and titles given to Jesus in Scripture clearly indicate who He is. There are so many, but we will only mention His main names and titles.

1. Jesus

Let us first consider His personal name, *Jesus*, which is the Greek form of the Old Testament name *Joshua*, meaning *Jehovah the Saviour* or *Jehovah saves*. Certainly His name expresses the idea of divine redemption, and for this reason He was named. As the angel told Joseph, "*You shall call His name Jesus, for He will save His people from their sins*" (Matthew 1:21).

Dr. Charles Rolls in his wonderful book series on the names and titles of Jesus Christ wrote:

> As a name, Jesus is more grandly honoured and more grievously hated, more acclaimed and more accused than any other. We find it imprinted over six

> hundred times on the pages of the four Gospels, and it is the most charming, consoling, comforting name by which our beloved Saviour is known (Charles J. Rolls, *The World's Greatest Name*, Loizeaux Brothers, Neptune, New Jersey, 1984, pg. 107).

Jesus is not just any name, for it carries with it all the power, authority, and glory of God.

Let us consider what is in His name. It is:

- a **saving name** (Matthew 1:21; Acts 4:12; Romans 10:13)
- a **healing name** (Acts 3:6,16; 4:7,10,30)
- a **delivering name** – with the authority of the name of Jesus, demons are cast out (Acts 16:18; Mark 16:16)
- a **name above every name** (Philippians 2:5-11; Ephesians 1:21)
- the **name with all the answers to prayer** (John 14:13,14; 15:16)
- a **name that accomplishes all of God's purposes**. The book of Acts is full of the use of His glorious name.

II. CHRIST

Now, Jesus is His personal name, but Christ is His official title – a title that describes His mission. It comes from the Greek, translated from the Hebrew word *Mashiach* (*Messiah* in English). The Hebrew root word is *mashach*, which means *anoint*. So *Messiah* literally means the *anointed one*. In the Old Testament, prophets, priests, and kings were anointed with oil to show their consecration to God, having been set apart for a specific purpose. Jesus was not anointed with oil, but was anointed from above with a divine anointing for the purpose of carrying out His divine mission of bringing the good news of salvation to the world (Luke 4:18; Acts 10:38).

Jesus was God's holy, anointed One, the Son of David, the rightful King who inherits the promise to David of a kingdom that will not end (Luke 1:32,33; cf. Isaiah 9:6,7; 2 Samuel 7:16). To refer to Jesus as the Son of David is the same as calling Him the Messiah, since a necessary qualification of the Messiah was His Davidic descent. However, the title Son of David is not a complete description of the Messiah, who is much more than just a human son. Prophetic Scripture clearly portrayed the divine nature of the Messiah (Isaiah 40:10; 42:13; Psalm 98:9).

The people in Jesus' day had ignored this aspect of the Messiah, and were instead looking for a man who would be a king like David. Knowing of this misconception, Jesus was careful, especially at the start of His ministry, that the people who followed Him would not try to make Him an earthly king. In an attempt to correct them, Jesus asked the Pharisees, who were the most religious and supposedly knew the Scriptures:

> *"What do you think about the Christ? Whose Son is He?" They said to Him, "The Son of David." He said to them, "How then does David in the Spirit call Him 'Lord,'...If David then calls Him 'Lord,' how is He his Son?"* (Matthew 22:42-45).

They were unable to answer Jesus' question because they did not fully understand what it meant to be the Messiah. The answer is that the Messiah is both the Son of David (since He was born of Mary), a descendant of David, and also David's Lord, since He is the Son of God.

Jesus accepted the title of Christ from His disciples (Mark 8:29), and during His triumphal entry into Jerusalem, He accepted the Messianic title, *"Son of David"* (Mark 11:1-10). At His trial before the Sanhedrin, when asked, *"Tell us if You are the Christ, the Son of God"* (Matthew 26:63), Jesus affirmed it to be true.

III. THE SON OF MAN

To continue this account of Jesus' trial, He also called Himself *"the Son of Man,"* which brings us to the third title. The high priest understood Jesus' words to claim divinity, and so he accused Jesus of blasphemy (Mark 14:61-64; Matthew 26:63-65). Why would the high priest be so upset when Jesus referred to Himself as *"the Son of Man"*? To understand, we must read from Daniel 7:13,14:

> *Behold, One like the Son of Man, coming with the clouds of heaven! ...Then to Him was given dominion and glory and a kingdom...which shall not pass away.*

Jesus specifically applied this prophecy to Himself and the high priest knew it. Jesus said to him,

> *Hereafter you will see the Son of Man sitting at the right hand of the Power, and coming on the clouds of heaven* (Matthew 26:64; cf. Matthew 16:28).

The Sanhedrin saw little difference between the claim to be the Son of God and the Son of Man (see Luke 22:67-70).

If a normal person said, "I am a son of man," the response would be, "Well, sure isn't everyone?!" But when Jesus referred to Himself as the Son of Man, it meant that He was different. He was the heavenly Man who came down from above to identify Himself with humanity, that He might be our Saviour. So when Jesus calls Himself Son of Man it indicates both His humanity and His deity, and also His earthly ministry, suffering, exaltation, Second Coming, and rule over humanity (Matthew 13:41; 24:27,30; 25:31; 26:24; Mark 8:31; Luke 18:8; 19:10; 21:36).

IV. The Son of God

This is a clear claim of deity, for it implies oneness with God, His pre-existent Sonship; and being born of God, indicating His supernatural conception. The people around Jesus understood it as a claim of deity, as did His adversaries who accused Him of blasphemy because of it (John 10:33,36).

This title shows Jesus' unique and special relationship with God, His Father. Jesus called Him, *"My Father"* (there are 104 recorded instances when Jesus spoke to His Father). The title, *Son of God,* indicates closeness and love (John 5:18). Jesus is the only Son, equal with God, and eternal with God. This topic is dealt with in more detail under the chapter, *Jesus Christ – the Son of God*, earlier in this book.

V. Lord

This title indicates His deity, sovereignty, and exaltation (Acts 2:36). The Greek word for *Lord* is *Kurios*. In the second and third centuries BC, when the Old Testament was translated into Greek (a version called the Septuagint), they used the word *Kurios* as a substitute for the most holy, sacred, personal, and unpronounceable name of God. It was represented by four Hebrew letters, equivalent to the letters *YHWH*, which we pronounce as *Jehovah* or *Yahweh*. Religious Jews, however, will not attempt to say this name, for it is too high and honourable to be uttered by human lips. Instead, they say the word *Adonai*, which is Hebrew for *Lord*. Therefore, when Jesus was called "*Lord*," it was, in most instances, a reference to His deity, for it is practically equivalent to the word, *God*. For example, when Thomas believed that Jesus was alive, he exclaimed: "*My Lord and my God!*" (John 20:28; Mark 12:36,37; Luke 2:11; 3:4; Acts 2:36; 1 Corinthians 12:3; Philippians 2:11; Joshua 3:11; Psalm 97:5). Yet the earliest confession of faith in the Christian church was likely "*Jesus is Lord*" (1 Corinthians 12:3; 2 Corinthians 4:5; Romans 10:9; Philippians 2:11).

Jesus identified Himself with Jehovah, the Lord. He used of Himself the personal name of God, *I AM* (Exodus 3:14; cf. John 8:24,58; 18:5,6; Mark 14:62). He also attributed to Himself the roles of *Jehovah, the Lord*, such as His great *I AM* claims of being the *Bread of Life*, the *Way*, and the *Light* (John 6:35; 8:12; 11:25; 14:6). Others are the *Bridegroom* (Isaiah 62:5; Ezekiel 16:8; cf. Mark 2:19; John 3:29; Revelation 19:7), the *Shepherd* (Psalm 23:1; Isaiah 40:11; Ezekiel 34:15; cf. John 10:11), and the *Glory of God* (John 12:41; Isaiah 6:1).

God revealed Himself to the children of Israel in Egypt as being their Deliverer and Saviour, and then He revealed Himself at Sinai to be their King and Lord (Exodus 20:2). He had every right to be their Lord since He saved them. Likewise, the Lord Jesus has saved us from sin and death, so He has the right to be Lord of our lives (1 Corinthians 6:20; 2 Corinthians 5:15). He is indeed the "*Lord of lords*" (1 Timothy 6:15). In Scripture, we read, "*For whoever calls upon the name of the Lord shall be saved*" (Romans 10:13). Call upon Him and serve Him, for He is the Lord!

Chapter 18

The Gospel of the Lord Jesus Christ

MY FIRST reaction when I think about the Gospel which literally means *Good News*, is that it puts a smile on my face. The Gospel has changed my life. To begin with, I want to declare, along with the Apostle Paul, *"I am not ashamed of the Gospel of Christ, for it is the power of God to salvation for everyone who believes"* (Romans 1:16). The *"power of God to salvation"!* This statement alone tells us of the Gospel's importance. In fact, the Gospel was and is the most important news that has ever been told on earth. It is a divine message for all humankind. A message the whole world must hear, since hearing and believing the Gospel is a matter of life or death – even life everlasting for those who believe.

The central message of the Gospel is the life, death, resurrection, and redemptive work of the Lord Jesus Christ (1 Corinthians 1:1-3). It is called in Scripture, *"the Gospel of Christ"* (1 Thessalonians 3:2; Romans 1:16;

15:19), *"the Gospel of God"* (Romans 1:1; 1 Thessalonians 2:2,8,9), *"the Gospel of Jesus Christ, the Son of God"* (Mark 1:1; Romans 1:9), and "the glorious Gospel of the blessed God" (1 Timothy 1:11). It is referred to as the *Gospel of belief*, the *Gospel of truth*, and the *Gospel of salvation* (Luke 3:6). The Gospel has life in it! It is the most unique message, since it is about the most unique person who ever walked this earth. No other person (Jesus Himself never wrote down anything He said) had so many people writing so much about Him and the great things He had spoken.

The Gospel is powerful! It brings deliverance, healing, freedom, joy, and the entrance to eternal life (Luke 4:18). Why is this Good News so powerful? Because it proclaims the great and marvellous truths of Jesus Christ.

As believers, according to Scripture, what is to be our response to the Gospel? We are to:

- believe in it (Mark 1:15)
- preach it (Mark 16:15; Matthew 24:14)
- endure persecution and hardship for the sake of it (2 Timothy 1:8; Philippians 1:12)
- give to those in ministry for the sake of it (Philippians 1:5)
- live according to it with unity (Philippians 1:27a)
- work hard and even struggle for the sake of proclaiming it (Philippians 1:27b)
- defend and establish it (Philippians 1:7)
- keep the pure Gospel and not pervert it (Galatians 1:6,7).

In Scripture, we are told that there are blessings of the Gospel (Romans 15:29). Paul was so filled with the Gospel that he called it *"my Gospel"* and explained it to be *"the revelation of the mystery"* (Romans 16:25) that came to him directly from Jesus Christ (Galatians 1:11).

The Gospel Writers

Four of Jesus' followers – Matthew, Mark, Luke, and John – wrote a detailed account of the Gospel. You should realize that these accounts are not four Gospels, as some might think, but rather, four records of one Gospel. That is why we say, the Gospel according to Matthew, or the Gospel according to Mark, and so on. The writers recorded their accounts from their own perspective. Certainly Matthew and John were eyewitnesses since they were among the 12 disciples chosen by Jesus. I have heard knowledgeable lawyers say that the different perspectives, and the seemingly slight and occasional differences in the accounts, attest to the truth of their testimony. If they had collaborated in their testimony, then suspicion would arise; but it is clear, however, that the Gospel accounts are not forgeries.

Each man wrote his Gospel account under the inspiration of the Spirit of God, thus it was a true account. Although God inspired them, He did not take away their individuality, their own writing styles, or their focus or perspective. For example, Matthew wrote to a Jewish audience, so he stressed the Messiahship and Kingship of Jesus. Mark wrote to a Roman audience and, therefore, omits the genealogy of Jesus and other references to Jewish customs, prophecy, and the Law. Many of the early Christians in Rome were servants, and thus Mark stresses the divine servanthood of Jesus and His role as the Redeemer (Mark 10:43-45).

Luke was a learned man. He was certainly an historian, and the Apostle Paul called him, *"the beloved physician"* (Colossians 4:14). He gears his Gospel account to the Greek audience – a mostly educated group who were interested in historical facts, as well as philosophy. Therefore, Luke gives the most complete chronological account of Jesus' life, while stressing the perfect humanity and compassion of Jesus, the Son of Man.

John was the last to write an account of the Gospel – probably written between 60 and 90 AD. He was likely the oldest and last surviving eyewitness of the Lord Jesus. Because John writes to a universal audience, he stresses the deity and incarnation of Jesus – the Son of God, the God-Man. By providing a more theological emphasis rather than an historical emphasis, we also know he is not as concerned about the chronology of events, but rather writes to instill faith in his readers. One of his intentions was to combat heresy that had been creeping into the church and to teach the pure Gospel. John clearly stated his intention in writing his Gospel account, saying,

> *But these are written that you may believe that Jesus is the Christ, the Son of God, and that believing you may have life in His name* (John 20:31).

The Spread of the Gospel

The Gospel of Jesus Christ did not come merely with words, but with signs and wonders which validated the message as authentic and divine. It was also readily accepted because of the righteous characters of the messengers. After Paul and his helpers boldly proclaimed the Gospel, even though there was much conflict, they established a church in Thessalonica. He wrote to them, saying,

> *For our Gospel did not come to you in word only, but also in power, and in the Holy Spirit and in much assurance, as you know what kind of men we were among you for your sake* (1 Thessalonians 1:5; 2:2,3).

From this, we learn how important it is for those carrying the Gospel message to be Christ-like. For how will people be drawn to follow Christ and believe in the Gospel, if His messengers are not righteous people who strive to live holy lives? It is an honour to preach the Gospel. As the Apostle Paul continued to tell the Thessalonians,

> *But as we have been approved by God to be entrusted with the Gospel, even so we speak, not as pleasing men, but God who tests our hearts* (1 Thessalonians 2:4).

They had the right motives in proclaiming the Gospel. They were not seeking material gain, but shared the Gospel because they loved the people and did not want them to be lost and die in their sin (1 Thessalonians 2:5-8). The Gospel of Jesus Christ is the only answer for the sin problem of this world. It affords us the solution, if we only believe.

Why must we preach the Gospel?

1. **Our Lord Jesus commanded us** to preach the Gospel, and we must obey His voice. "*Go into all the world and preach the Gospel to every creature*" (Mark 16:15).
2. ***"How shall they hear without a preacher?"*** (Romans 10:14b). This is the only way to reach people, for "*faith comes by hearing, and hearing by the word of God*" (Romans 10:17).

3. **It is the ultimate Good News** (1 Corinthians 15:1-14; Luke 4:18).
   - life out of death (John 5:24)
   - light out of darkness (Acts 26:16-18; Colossians 1:13)
   - hope out of despair (Colossians 1:27,28)
   - satisfaction out of need (2 Corinthians 8:9; Philippians 4:19)
   - healing from disease (1 Peter 2:24; Matthew 8:16,17; Mark 16:16-18)
   - freedom from slavery and oppression (John 8:35,36)
   - redemption because of the cross (1 Corinthians 1:23,24; 2:4,5; 1 Peter 1:18-20).
4. ***"The Lord is...not willing that any should perish but that all should come to repentance"*** (2 Peter 3:9). Hell is for Satan and his demons; it is not intended for humankind.
5. **Only Jesus offers the answers to the world**, and through the Gospel we find love, joy, peace, hope, security, and salvation (Luke 19:10; John 10:10; Acts 4:12; Romans 5:1).
6. **Jesus died for all precious souls.** He demonstrated His love and gave up His life for them (Romans 5:8; John 3:16,17).
7. **The love of Jesus within us for the lost constrains us** (2 Corinthians 5:14,15).
8. **The judgement and wrath of God will come upon unbelievers** (Romans 1:16,18; 2:4-6,11; John 3:18-21; Hebrews 10:31).

9. **The time is coming when it will be more difficult** (2 Timothy 4:2-5; John 9:4). We must preach at all times and take advantage of the time now.

10. **Jesus is coming back soon,** and thereafter, it will be too late (Matthew 24:14).

Take the opportunity given to you now, and believe the wonderful Gospel message of Jesus Christ. If you are already a believer, then I encourage you to share the Gospel with someone today. It is the most fulfilling thing you can ever do!

Chapter 19

The Cost of Following Jesus

ALTHOUGH salvation through the redemptive work of Jesus Christ is a free gift of God's grace, it does not come cheaply. It cost Jesus His life, and for some believers, it has cost them their lives. Jesus did not hide the fact that following Him would not be an easy road. He clearly said that those who follow Him would face persecution (Mark 21:12). He did not ask His followers to endure something He did not, nor could not, endure. For some people, actually for the majority, this notion causes them to leave Jesus (John 6:60,66); but the true, strong believer will follow Jesus despite persecution. They, in fact, will rejoice in persecution (Matthew 5:11,12; 2 Corinthians 12:10), like Paul, knowing that His service has not been in vain and that he is counted worthy of sharing with Christ in His suffering (Philippians 3:10). It takes full commitment, which is what Jesus demands of His followers.

When Jesus began His public ministry on earth, He chose 12 men to be His disciples. *Disciple* means *a learner*.

Interestingly, He did not select the learned men or the religious leaders of His day. Rather, He chose simple, tough, hard-working men from different backgrounds and even different personalities and characteristics. They were men who, in the natural, would seem the least likely to be chosen as disciples. Jesus chose unlearned fishermen, and even a cold-hearted tax collector, who the people saw as a collaborator with their Roman oppressors. He even chose hot-headed, rowdy youths, James and John, nicknamed "sons of thunder." Also, He chose a political activist, Simon the Zealot, whom the Romans would have labelled a terrorist. Jesus, however, saw beyond the natural. He saw their hearts. He knew that Nathanael was a "true Israelite" because his heart was truthful. Jesus saw their potential, just as He sees potential in you, and thus is calling you to likewise follow Him.

The disciples were divinely chosen by God who shaped them, moulded them, equipped them, empowered them, and then sent them out on a divine mission. They later came to be known as *apostles,* meaning *sent ones*, and they became the pillars of the church. These dedicated men of God counted the cost and decided that, despite persecution and even death, it was worth it to follow Jesus.

At the height of Jesus' popularity, He explained to the crowds that there was a cost in following Him. His strong and straightforward words are recorded in Luke 14:25-35. These words must have disappointed many people in the crowd, for after learning of this and other things they did not want to hear, many lost interest and left Jesus, content to live the way they always had. But the ones who had wholly dedicated themselves to Jesus remained steadfast. In the Scriptures, we read,

> *Then Jesus said to the twelve, "Do you also want to go away?" Then Simon Peter answered Him, "Lord, to whom shall we go? You have the words of eternal life. Also we have come to believe and know that You are the Christ, the Son of the living God"* (John 6:67-69).

Since Peter had discovered the truth and believed on Jesus, he did not want to go back to the place he was before personally encountering the Saviour. He and the other disciples, except Judas, were willing to bear the cost of following Jesus.

What is the cost of discipleship? A true follower must:

1. **Leave everything to follow Jesus**, meaning that He must have first priority in our lives over anything or anyone else.

2. **Deny oneself.** To do the will of Jesus is to be more important that our own selfish ambitions and desires. We should pray, not my will, but Yours be done.

3. **Follow Him unconditionally**, and not let the concerns of this world prevent us. A total separation from worldliness and a total commitment to Jesus is required. In Luke 9:57-62, we read of three people who desired to be disciples of Jesus, but their priorities were not right. Jesus required their undivided attention and loyalty, but they were more concerned with possessions, personal gain, their livelihood, and families. A person who does not put Jesus first cannot be a true follower.

4. **Love Him supremely** with our whole heart, even more than we love ourselves and those closest to us. Jesus said,

He who loves father or mother more than Me is not worthy of Me. And he who loves son or daughter more than Me is not worthy of Me (Matthew 10:37).

In comparison to the love we have for Jesus, it is like hating those who, in the natural sense, are closest to us (Luke 14:26). This does not mean we do not love our family members; rather, Jesus used this expression as a means of comparison.

5. **Be willing to sacrifice** for the sake of following Jesus. There may be a heavy price we must pay to follow Him with utmost commitment. For some, it may mean giving up extra income or comforts, even giving up position, honour or reputation. Let us have the attitude of the Apostle Paul who said,

   But indeed I also count all things loss for the excellence of the knowledge of Christ Jesus my Lord, for whom I have suffered the loss of all things, and count them as rubbish, that I may gain Christ (Philippians 3:8).

6. **Count the cost, and consider the hardships** that will arise for the sake of Jesus. It could cause much division in the home, if one or two are believers in Jesus and the others are not. With this scenario in mind, Jesus said,

   Do you suppose that I came to give peace on earth? I tell you, not at all, but rather division. For from now on five in one house will be divided: three against two, and two against three. Father will be divided against son and son against father, mother against daughter and daughter against mother... (Luke 12:51-53).

Converts to Christianity from other religions have experienced division and have even been abandoned and cast out by their families (Matthew 24:9). For them, there is no peace on earth, and yet they do have peace in their hearts, for they have peace with God and one day will have peace in eternity with God.

7. **Have total surrender** (Luke 14:33) and undying allegiance. We are to follow Jesus always, going wherever He leads and obeying His every command. He commands that we repent of sin, submit our wills, renew our minds, be baptized, consecrate our hearts, worship Him, and have full and complete obedience to Him.

8. **Keep His commandments**, be willing to submit to Him, and live a life worthy of bearing His name, that of being a "Christian." Jesus said, *"If you love Me, keep My commandments"* (John 14:15). Every aspect of our lives must be God-honouring.

9. ***"Bear [carry] his cross"* and follow Jesus** (Luke 14:27). This means that we must endure pain, suffering, persecution (Philippians 1:29), and even be willing to die for Him. The Apostle Paul exhorted the young man Timothy, *"You therefore must endure hardship as a good soldier of Jesus Christ"* (2 Timothy 2:3).

In Western society, Christians do not face persecution as some believers do in other parts of the world – like those who endure torture, imprisonment, and death. Christians can, however, be attacked mentally and emotionally, being bombarded by secular humanism, evolution, and other worldly ways at every turn. We must guard our minds, for Satan tries in subtle ways to draw us away from the true path of following Jesus.

What are the reasons that followers of Jesus face persecution?

- The persecutors are used by Satan to **discourage people from looking to God** and finding the truth.
- The persecutors **do not love the truth.**
- The persecutors **love darkness** (John 3:18-21).
- Jesus said His followers are persecuted and will be persecuted **for His name's sake** (Matthew 10:22; 24:9; Mark 13:13).
- Jesus said they are persecuted **for righteousness' sake.**

The people in the world who have faced the most persecution throughout history are Christians. In fact, today, more than any other time in history, Christians are being persecuted. One of the signs that we are followers of Jesus is that we love and help our fellow Christians (Hebrews 13:3; Matthew 25:36). I encourage you to get involved in ways that will help the persecuted church. Support organizations that aid persecuted Christians, such as the ministries of Voice of the Martyrs and Open Doors, founded by Brother Andrew.

Jesus was so full of love that He was the greatest champion of human rights. He elevated the rights of children and women, for inherent in Christianity is human dignity, freedom of choice, and non-violence. If governments and society would only follow the teachings of Jesus, what an improvement we would see! The Bible teaches that one day each individual and even countries as a whole, will stand before God to give an account. His judgements will be final and just. Therefore, I encourage you to follow Jesus with your whole heart.

What are the benefits and promises of Jesus when you follow Him?

1. **It is the only way to please God.**

2. **It is the only way to eternal life.**

3. **He will give us His authority.**

4. **His presence will always be with us.** He has promised to never leave us nor forsake us, even when our family forsakes us (Luke 21:16-18).

5. **He will give us the words to speak and wisdom to answer** (Mark 13:11; Luke 21:15). We will be like lambs among wolves, as gentle as doves, and as wise as serpents (Matthew 10:16-20).

6. **We will be conquerors,** enduring persecution and having victory over Satan and sin by living for God, obeying Him, serving Him, loving Him, as well as loving others (Romans 8:35-39).

You must realize that to be a Christian takes a full commitment and that the path will not always be easy. However, it will always be rewarding, both in this life and in the life to come. A Christian is called to love and obey Jesus Christ above all others, even if it means losing our lives. As the Apostle Paul said, *"For to me, to live is Christ, and to die is gain"* (Philippians 1:21). My intent is not to discourage anyone, but to honestly tell you the real cost of following Jesus. Whatever the cost, it is worth it! I urge you to follow Christ today with your whole heart.

Chapter 20

Jesus and Social Justice: Part 1

THE WORLD's most compassionate person was our Lord Jesus Christ, for He had divine love for everyone, regardless of race, gender or social standing. His example, words, and deeds proved Him to be not only holy, but perfectly just.

Every man, woman, boy, and girl is equally important, extremely valuable, and precious in God's sight. We are all created in His image (Genesis 1:26,27) and are the crown of all creation. The fact that we are the object of His care and love was expressed in the greatest way through His wonderful plan of redemption. Jesus came into the world, lived among us, and died as a sacrifice for our sins to bring us into right relationship with God. Sin had destroyed this relationship, but *"God was in Christ reconciling the world to Himself"* (2 Corinthians 5:19).

Jesus Met Individual Needs

God, our Creator, knows what we need, and Jesus

became the answer for those needs. When it comes to the essential needs, all humankind is alike, for we all have physical, social, and emotional needs. But the most important need that is often overlooked is our spiritual need. Our ultimate purpose in life is to be in right relationship with God – to praise Him, honour Him, and please Him – and when we do, God takes delight and pleasure in us.

From studying the life of Jesus, we can clearly see the divine love He had for everyone. It is also evident that Jesus moved about with a divine plan. Wherever He went, He met the people's needs, be it physical, mental, emotional or spiritual. Jesus always *"went about doing good"* (Acts 10:38; Luke 4:18). On two separate occasions (as mentioned earlier in this book), He saw the need, had compassion, and fed thousands of people (John 6). He had the solution to His and Peter's need to pay their taxes by providing the necessary coin from the mouth of a fish (Matthew 17:27). He saved the wedding hosts from great social embarrassment by providing them with more wine (John 2:1-11). He even turned funerals into occasions for joy, for He came to give joy and life in abundance (John 10:10).

Every Individual is of Equal Importance

Each individual is extremely important to Jesus, and from Scripture we learn that He treated everyone alike. In His society, not all people were considered equal, but Jesus elevated everyone to an equal position of respect. He broke down the barriers between man and woman, slave and free, Jew and Gentile (Ephesians 2:14,18; Galatians 3:26-28). In Christ, we are all one. His disciple Peter, after spending three years under his teachings, could confidently proclaim:

In truth I perceive that God shows no partiality. But in every nation whoever fears Him and works righteousness is accepted by Him.... He is Lord of all... (Acts 10:34-36).

The Lord Jesus was a great champion of human rights and there are many examples in the Gospel records of this. He championed the rights of:

- children
- women
- foreigners (He cleared the merchants out of the temple court which was the area where the Gentiles could gather to pray)
- slaves and prisoners
- the oppressed and persecuted, such as the woman caught in adultery who could not defend herself (John 8:1-11).

Although Jesus first came to the lost sheep of Israel, it was His desire that through them, the Gospel would reach the rest of the world. Yet He still had several dealings with Gentiles. Jesus praised the faith of two Gentiles – the Canaanite woman (Matthew 15:28) and the Roman centurion whose faith, He said, was greater than any of his countrymen (Luke 7:9). To bring a balance, Jesus exposed the hypocrisy and lack of faith of the so-called great religious men. Although they were the most respected and honoured people in His day, in reality, they were the most prejudiced and the cause of many problems.

Jesus, however, treated all people with dignity. He welcomed everyone, even little children, to come to Him, just as He does today. Jesus stressed the need to care for prisoners, knowing that many had been mistreated and unjustly condemned. He took special care of orphans and widows. He saw the need of the widow in Nain, and raised to life her only son who would have been her sole source of income. He cared for the downtrodden and outcasts, like the woman at the well in Samaria (John 4) and reached out to the unwanted and untouchables of society, such as the lepers. He cared for the poor. He ignored the prejudice of His day, and associated with tax collectors and other *"sinners"* (Matthew 9:10; 11:19). Even on His way to Jerusalem, where He knew He would suffer and die on the cross, He took the time to stop in Jericho to bring salvation to Zacchaeus. This man was among the most despised of society – the tax collectors, who were considered collaborators with the Romans (Luke 19:1-10). Jesus also took the time to heal the poor beggar's blinded eyes, and thus gave him the chance to work and live a normal life (Luke 18:35-43). While in Jerusalem, He saw and commended the poor widow who gave all she had to God. Even though it was a very small amount, He said it was more than all the gold that the others gave (Luke 21:1-4).

Clearly, Jesus was a radical. He was not content to go along with society's ideas or prejudices, or with their social or racial profiling.

Not a Political Agenda

Jesus did not come for a political purpose or to destroy the Roman oppressors. He was wise and did not fall into His enemies' traps of breaking the Roman law or speaking against them. He did not consent to the people's desire to make Him king, and since He did not have a political agenda, many of His early followers left Him. His intent was not to change the political situation or bring reformation, but rather to show the love of God and bring transformation by changing the hearts of individuals and turning them to God.

So many Christians today, and throughout history, have lost the proper focus. Christians are to be like Jesus, so our focus should be like that of Jesus. We are to be merciful, and we are to be peacemakers. Jesus said:

> *Blessed are the merciful, for they shall obtain mercy. Blessed are the pure in heart, for they shall see God. Blessed are the peacemakers, for they shall be called sons of God. Blessed are those who are persecuted for righteousness' sake, for theirs is the kingdom of heaven* (Matthew 5:7-10).

We must not lose our sense of purpose nor compromise moral principles to be "politically correct." It is not our role as Christians to become so political that we lose focus on the needs of individuals or blindly take sides. Taking sides results in partiality and a lack of sensitivity to the other side, causing hurt and deep wounds. Standing on the side of justice, however, is more important than anyone's political or even theological ideologies. Let us show the love of Jesus by praying for the persecuted, caring for the needy, opposing racism, and upholding the dignity of all humankind. In my study of Scripture, I have seen repeatedly the exhortation for Christians to care for the needs of fellow believers. For just as we would help a brother or sister, so, too, are we obliged, as members of the family of God, to help our brothers and sisters in the Lord (Galatians 6:2,9,10; Romans 12:13).

Jesus, Our Role Model

The motto for the Christian should be as the Apostle Paul expressed: *"I have been crucified with Christ; it is no longer I who live, but Christ lives in me"* (Galatians 2:20). And John, Jesus' beloved disciple, admonished the believer, saying, *"He who says he abides in Him ought himself also to walk just as He walked"* (1 John 2:6; Romans 8:29). Speaking of rights, because of who Jesus is and because of what He has accomplished on the cross, He has the right to be our Lord and Role Model.

Sadly, many so-called Christian countries have done just the opposite of what Jesus would have done, such as the many evils of colonialism and slavery, the evils of the Holocaust in Europe, and farther back to the evils of the crusades – things which brought damage and shame.

There is no such thing as a "Christian country"; there is only the kingdom of God which has no geographical boundaries, and consists of individuals from all backgrounds, languages, and ethnic groups. This includes people who have enthroned Jesus as Lord over their lives, abide by His teaching, and strive to live up to His example. You will find even in countries that adhere to atheism, are closed to Christianity, and hostile to the Gospel message, many Christians are still living there. Their true citizenship is in heaven, their true nation is the kingdom of God, and their true family is the family of God, for they are considered the people of God, the true children of Abraham. Jesus showed this distinction when He said of Nathanael, *"Here is a true Israelite."* Now Nathanael was already an Israelite, but Jesus made the distinction because of his pure heart, and the fact that he believed in Him. This is what made him a "true Israelite" and a member of God's kingdom.

Jesus declared many times that the kingdom of God is for the poor and oppressed, the weak and downtrodden, the sick, and those who cannot support or defend themselves. These people have a special place in God's heart and they are the ones for whom Jesus came.

Chapter 21

Jesus and Social Justice Part 2

LET US look at specific instances in the Gospel records of the ways in which Jesus was a champion of human rights, and a strong proponent of social justice. He certainly stands unique in this respect, and He did things and said things that were unheard of in His day and age. His teachings were radical and caused the birth of a whole new way of thinking or mindset, which came to be the mark of the Christian community. One of the most radical teachings of Jesus was to love your enemies and do good to those who wrongfully use you (Matthew 5:44). This concept could not be understood by a society that trampled on the weak and defenceless, and considered wealthy men to be superior to all others. *"By this all will know that you are My disciples, if you have love for one another"* (John 13:35). The early church lived in unity and took care of each other – the wealthier helping those in need (Acts 4:32-35). They especially cared for widows and orphans, since Jesus had in many ways shown His love and concern for widows and had come to be a Father to the fatherless.

Jesus Championed the Rights of Women

The segment of society in Jesus' day considered among the lowest were women, but Jesus was a champion for women's rights. He gave great value, importance, and respect to women who were often mistreated and thought of as inferior or second-class citizens. He stressed very strongly to the men that it was God's intention from the beginning for there to be one man and one woman united in marriage, and that the two should be as one (Matthew 19:3-6). In other words, a woman was not to be a possession or an object that a man could do with as he wished. Rather, she was a person who was just as important as a man; after all, this is the only way they could be united and become one flesh.

Throughout the Gospel accounts, especially Luke's record, we see the great role that women had in the life of Jesus. There was Mary, His mother, whom God greatly favoured, and to whom Jesus was submissive and held in the highest respect. Even while upon the cross, Jesus showed His great love and concern for Mary by asking His beloved friend and disciple, John, to take care of her, as though she were his own mother.

Jesus had a close friendship with the sisters Mary and Martha of Bethany, and when he taught and spoke to His inner circle, their presence was welcomed. Mary, in particular, enjoyed listening to Jesus and learning from Him. Jesus certainly did not insult the woman's intelligence, as would other rabbis of His day; for at that time, it was only boys and men who were schooled.

There were other women who were followers of Jesus and who enjoyed His company, and He certainly was never condescending to them. They stayed with Jesus to the very end when He was upon the cross, and even afterwards, when He was in the tomb, they went to honour Him. In fact, Jesus first appeared to the women after He had risen from the dead.

In His ministry, Jesus paid much attention to the needs of women. While Jesus was on His way with a leader of the community to heal his daughter, a sick woman touched Him. Jesus stopped, kept the important man anxiously waiting, enquired after the woman who had touched Him, then spoke kindly to her: *"Daughter, be of good cheer; your faith has made you well. Go in peace"* (Luke 8:48). With this delay, the man's daughter had died, but Jesus told him to only believe and she would be well (Luke 8:50). The Lord tenderly spoke words of life and the little girl arose from the dead (Luke 8:54,55).

Jesus treated women in the same way he treated men. He spent time talking at the well with the despised, rejected, and divorced Samaritan woman (John 4:5-26) who was an outcast from both her society and His. She was of a different nationality, and the Jews were prejudiced against the Samaritans. Yet to Jesus she was precious, important, and worthy of His time and love.

When Jesus healed the woman whose back was misshapen and bent over, He called her a *"daughter of Abraham."* Now the Jews would always boast that they were *"sons of Abraham,"* but Jesus put her on the same level of importance as a son, by calling her a *"daughter of Abraham"* (Luke 13:10-17).

In another instance, Jesus protected and defended the woman caught in adultery. It wasn't right that the mob was just going after the woman, for obviously there had to have been a man involved too. This also shows their discrimination against women. Whatever Jesus wrote on the ground, it caused the men with stones in their hands to drop them and depart. Jesus showed mercy and forgiveness, yet He was firm in telling her to go and sin no more (John 8:1-11).

Jesus Championed the Rights of Children

Like the women in Jesus' day, children (especially girls), were considered less important, but Jesus did not share this view. He gave children His time, attention, and care. He raised a little girl who had died back to life and He honoured the faith of a boy who gave His lunch to Jesus. Plus, there are many other instances where Jesus elevated children to a place of importance. I have devoted a chapter in this book about Jesus and children, geared especially to children. I encourage you to read this chapter to your children or others you know. They need to understand how important they are to the Lord Jesus. The disciples of Jesus learned this lesson when He rebuked them for trying to keep the children away from Him. He wanted them to come to Him and He blessed each one (Mark 10:13-16).

Jesus Fought Racism

Jesus was not prejudiced against anyone. Most people of His nation and religion thought of themselves as superior. Had they forgotten that God chose them, not because of their own merit, but simply because of love and as a means to bless the whole world, which was fulfilled through Jesus? (Deuteronomy 7:7; Genesis 22:17).

From Jesus' example, it is evident that in the kingdom of God there is no place for racism. Those who despise others are despising God, for every person is of equal value and created in His image. Jesus came to destroy the barriers and walls between people. No matter what their background or nationality, no one is superior to another. Although Jesus began His ministry among His own people, whom He called *"the lost sheep of Israel,"* it was His intention for the whole world to hear His Good News message. That is why He commanded His followers to go into all the world with the Gospel to every nation.

Jesus actually offended some of the Jews by elevating people of other nationalities to places of importance, such as when He preached in Nazareth. There, He gave two examples of God-fearing Gentiles and their association with the great prophets, Elijah and Elisha (Luke 4:24-28). God blessed these Gentiles from the regions of Lebanon and Syria. Still today, God loves the people from these regions and from all countries, and He desires to bless everyone through His Son Jesus.

Another example of Jesus' shocking lack of prejudice is found in His story of the Good Samaritan. Jesus elevated the Samaritan – a nationality that the Jews despised. He showed the Samaritan to be the most righteous since the man extended mercy and cared for the needy without receiving any recompense or reward (Luke 10:29-37). Even Jesus' speaking with the Samaritan woman at the well was against His culture; but for the sake of love and for her salvation, Jesus transcended His culture and the norm of His day.

A true follower of Jesus cannot be a racist. We are to love each person, as does our Lord, regardless of one's national origin, colour of skin, religion or beliefs. I am hesitant to use the word "race," since in actuality, we are all of the same race – the human race. There is really only one race, and that is the way we should consider all people – the same.

The Problem of Wealth

Another area of social justice that Jesus spoke much about is the area of wealth and its distribution. He condemned those who trusted in money; whose goal in life was to accumulate as much wealth as they could. For to these types of people, money is their god. Jesus said to His followers, *"But seek the kingdom of God, and all these things shall be added to you."* And He continued to say, *"For where your treasure is, there your heart will be also"* (Luke 12:31,34).

Jesus told the parable of the rich fool after warning two brothers who were quarrelling over their inheritance. Jesus warned:

> *Take heed and beware of covetousness, for one's life does not consist in the abundance of the things he possesses* (Luke 12:15).

The parable that followed showed the folly of selfishly gathering wealth and not sharing or being charitable (Luke 12:16-21).

Selfishness is one of the main reasons for war. People have died for the sake of having a few more metres of land or to gain another person's or another country's wealth. If we lived by the teachings of Jesus, there would be no wars or contentions. In many countries, there is a marked imbalance of wealth where most of the country's wealth is in the hands of a few. These are the countries whose governments are the most corrupt. They crush the poor, and the poor become poorer so the rich can get richer and more powerful at the expense of the weak.

In Scripture, we read, *"For the love of money is a root of all kinds of evil"* (1 Timothy 6:10; 6:7-9). If people were not greedy, and treated others equally, then much of the social injustices in this world would be rectified. If the wealth of the world was evenly distributed, there would not be one starving child. Now, I realize that it is impossible to evenly distribute the wealth of the world. Jesus recognized this fact too by saying, *"For the poor you have with you always"* (John 12:8). Surely, the richer countries could do more to help the third world countries, and do more to save the lives of children who are dying every minute because of starvation. I applaud such charities as World Vision and encourage more people to become child sponsors. If the wealthier countries spent as much on humanitarian aid, as they do on their own military or even the military aid they give other countries, then the world would be in a much better situation. Much war, terrorism, and unrest could be avoided if only the people's needs were being met. On several occasions, Jesus exhorted people to give alms to the poor (Luke 11:41; 12:33; Matthew 6:3,4), for the poor had a special place in His heart.

As a test of love and commitment, Jesus asked the wealthy young man to sell all he had, give it to the poor, and then come and follow Him. Sadly, the young man was unwilling to do this. His money meant too much to him. This is one of the reasons, Jesus said it is hard, but not impossible, for a rich man to enter the kingdom of heaven (Matthew 19:16-26). There are other examples, however, of people in the early church who actually did sell all they had and gave it to the poor. I don't believe God has called all the wealthy to do this; but He does require them to hold their money lightly, to use it wisely as good stewards, to use it hospitably, charitably, and for the furtherance of His kingdom. This is the only way a person can *"lay up...treasures in heaven"* (Matthew 6:20).

The Inescapable Judgement

Here in this world, the justice system is incomplete and imperfect, for as is evident, the world remains filled with injustice and evil. The prisons are filled with many innocent people and many guilty are still free. Minorities are abused. Persecution and racism abound. Basic human rights are denied to many. Shamefully, much abuse and injustices are done in the name of God and for the sake of religion. In this present age, it appears that the ruthless and powerful are ruling, but at the end of this age, truth and true justice will prevail and the Lord Jesus will reign supreme. Every country and every man and woman will stand to be judged before a just and holy God (John 5:27-30; Matthew 25:31-46). For the unjust, it will be a fearful day (Matthew 23:33); but for the righteous, whose sins have been washed away by the blood of the Lamb – our Lord Jesus – it will be a day of encouragement and vindication.

Everything we do now in this life has eternal value. Let us remember to model Jesus with our words, deeds, and even our concern for social justice in this world.

Chapter 22

Jesus and Children (A Teaching Geared Specifically to Children)

THERE IS a story in the Bible that shows us how much Jesus loved children, and how important they are to Him. Let's read it:

> *People were bringing little children to Jesus. They wanted Him to touch them. But the disciples told the people to stop. When Jesus saw this, He was angry. He said to His disciples, "Let the little children come to Me. Don't keep them away. God's kingdom belongs to people like them. What I'm about to tell you is true. Anyone who will not receive God's kingdom like a little child will never enter it." Then He took the children into His arms. He put His hands on them and blessed them* (Mark 10:13-16 NIRV).

I have a baby named Nathaniel. I love to get down on the floor and play with him. I think this is just what Jesus did when the children came to Him. Jesus was so kind, good, and warm-hearted that all the children loved Him, and they knew that He loved them too. In the days of the Bible, it was the custom for the father of a child to lay his hands upon the child's head and say a blessing over him. Jesus was acting like a father when He blessed the children. In fact, I bless my own children in this same way.

Special words are usually said when a child is being blessed. One of the Biblical blessings goes like this:

> *The Lord bless you and keep you; the Lord make His face shine upon you, and be gracious to you; the Lord lift up His countenance upon you, and give you peace* (Numbers 6:24-26).

Maybe some of you have heard the minister say these words at the end of a church service. Maybe Jesus said words like this when He blessed the children.

I find it surprising that Jesus' disciples did not want the children to go to Him. Had they forgotten that Jesus had just taught them to welcome children? When He was teaching them about humility, being like a servant, and thinking of others as more important than themselves, He took a little child, held him in His arms, and told the disciples, *"Anyone who welcomes one of these little children in My name welcomes Me"* (Mark 9:37 NIRV). And Jesus also warned adults not to cause any child to stumble, or to be the reason that they would sin (Mark 9:42).

Maybe the disciples didn't think the children were important enough for Jesus to take time with them? After all, many important men, like the religious leaders, were coming up to Jesus and asking Him questions. Maybe they thought Jesus had more important things to do, or maybe it had been a long day and they didn't want Jesus to get tired out? But Jesus was angry at His disciples when they tried to stop the children from coming. Jesus cares so much about children, and He was very serious with His disciples about not hurting their feelings. The disciples had a wrong attitude about children, which may have been the way most people back in those days thought of them. But Jesus knew that children were just as important as adults. In fact, Jesus did not leave that place until He had held and blessed all the children that came to Him. I'm sure there were many, especially since in those days people had several children. They were thought of as gifts and blessings from God, and they still are a blessing. I have had six such blessings – Sarah, Hannah, David, Mary, Rebekah, and Nathaniel.

Jesus knew that children were very special and important. He took the time to hold them, laugh with them, play with them, and pray for them. It is no wonder the children loved Jesus and flocked around Him.

When Jesus was with the children, He took this opportunity to teach His disciples an important lesson about the kingdom of God. He told them that in order for a person to enter into the kingdom of God, or be a part of God's family, you first have to be like a child. Adults can learn a lot from children. Jesus didn't explain to His disciples exactly what He meant. But it can be easily understood, for innocent child-like qualities are spoken of in many other places in the Bible.

In what ways does Jesus want adults to be like children? He wants them to:

1. **Have humility**, like a little child who does not think he is better than anyone else.

2. **Have faith** like a child who believes that his parents will take care of him, feed him, clothe him, and love him always. This is how we are to think of God, our Heavenly Father.

3. **Trust**, as a little child trusts his parents and believes what they say is true. We are to trust in God and in the truth of His Word, the Bible.

4. **Have honesty**, like that of a little child. Everyone knows, sometimes to the embarrassment of their parents, that little children tell it just like it is. They are honest, and have complete sincerity.

5. **Be totally dependent on God for everything.** Little children have total dependency on their parents to take care of them, or else they could die. We have to depend on God's grace and mercy to be saved, forgiven of our sins, and for eternal life. Also, when a child gets hurt or has a problem, what do they do? They go directly to their parents for help. Likewise, when we have a need, God wants us to go to Him for help, for He is ready, willing, and able to help us with any problems we may face.

6. **Not feel inferior.** When I asked my eight-year-old daughter, Rebekah, what she thought Jesus wanted adults to learn from children, she answered, "Not thinking you're not good enough." And that is so true. Young children accept themselves just as they are and they don't have what is sometimes called an inferiority complex. God accepts us just as we are. There is nobody so bad that they can't come to Jesus and be loved, welcomed, and forgiven.

7. **Have the same openness and receptivity** like a child who gladly accepts a gift without having done anything to get it. Our salvation is a gift from God. We can't work for it, but we should gladly and openly receive it.

8. **Be full of wonder, amazement, and excitement** about learning and about life experiences. The children of Jerusalem were very excited and sang praises to Jesus when He entered the city. Adults should have this same sense of happiness, joy, and wonder when it comes to God, His goodness and His love.

While Jesus walked on the earth and ministered, there were many times He was with children. There was one special little boy who offered to share his lunch with Jesus, and from this small amount of food, Jesus multiplied it and fed thousands of people. He also healed a lot of sick children, and even brought a little girl who had died back to life! Jesus is the Life-Giver and our Creator because He is God. He alone has the power to give us eternal life with Him in heaven, if we only believe in Him. Thank you, children, for having such great qualities, and I hope and pray that as you grow up, you will always remember that in many ways you should stay like a child.

Chapter 23

THE SALVATION OF JESUS CHRIST

SALVATION is a great, spiritual work of God accomplished through our Lord Jesus Christ. The message of salvation was central to Jesus' teaching and it was a major subject of preaching by the apostles. It was also a central theme in the Old Testament writings and prophecies. The salvation of humankind was the primary reason that Jesus came into the world. As the angel told Joseph, Mary's husband,

> *And she will bring forth a Son, and you shall call His name Jesus, for He will save His people from their sins* (Matthew 1:21).

Theologians have written volumes on this subject and call it soteriology, or the doctrine of salvation. It is simple enough to even be understood and experienced by children. God has a definite plan, purpose, and method of accomplishing salvation. Let us consider what is involved, and this we learn from divine revelation in the Word of God.

The Condition of Humankind

Clearly, humankind is in dire need of salvation – salvation from sin, the power and influence of sin, the guilt of sin, and the penalty of sin which results in spiritual death and separation from God (Ephesians 2:1). As the Word of God reveals, every person is by nature sinful and guilty before God (Psalm 51:5; Isaiah 53:6). In Scripture, we read, *"For all have sinned and fall short of the glory of God"* (Romans 3:23; Galatians 3:22). Even without a knowledge of the Bible, it is inherent in human consciousness that we are sinful. Throughout history, people have felt this guilt which caused them to seek the remedy, resulting in the emergence of numerous religions.

Interestingly, in ancient religions, they all felt the need for there to be a sacrifice and spilling of blood to appease their deity. From the Word of God, we learn that there is only one way whereby a person can be saved (Acts 4:12; John 14:6). This way was determined before the foundation of the world. God foreknew that humankind would fall into sin, yet He still created us for His glory (Isaiah 43:7). He had a wonderful plan to offer salvation from sin to the whole world. One of the most famous and memorized verses of the Bible clearly explains it:

> *For God so loved the world that He gave His only begotten Son, that whoever believes in Him should not perish but have everlasting life* (John 3:16; 3:17).

God's Plan

How exactly did God provide this salvation which leads to everlasting life? As John 3:16 explains, He was moved by love and grace to send His Son Jesus into the world to become a Man. This is what we celebrate at the Christmas season; but to complete the picture, we must remember the reason for His birth. He came to die a sacrificial death in our place. In the latter part of Hebrews 9:26, we read, *"He has appeared to put away sin by the sacrifice of Himself."* This is the reason He is called *"the Lamb of God"* (John 1:29), the perfect, unblemished and sacrificial Lamb, foreshadowed by all the inadequate Old Testament animal sacrifices (Hebrews 9:12-14; 10:4,5). Jesus, the Perfect Sacrifice that God required, became human in order to die for the sins of humankind (Hebrews 2:9; 1 Peter 1:18-20; 1 John 3:5; 2 Corinthians 5:21). This is called the vicarious death, for Jesus died as a substitute and in our place. He took our sin upon Himself (1 Peter 2:24), and by His death, paid the penalty that the justice of God demanded.

A vital part of God's plan was for Jesus to defeat Satan (1 John 3:8; Colossians 2:15); triumph over the grave; rise from the dead; ascend to God, the Father; receive the power, honour, and rightful place on the throne; and intercede on our behalf (1 Timothy 3:16; Hebrews 1:1-4; 2:9; 1 John 2:1,2). When Jesus Christ returns, He will complete the good work He began in the lives and hearts of those who believe in Him. Ultimately, when the believer enjoys the blessed promise of eternal life in heaven with the Lord, we will have salvation from the presence of sin (Titus 2:11-14; Romans 12:11).

Humankind's Response

We have learned of God's plan of salvation, and that it is His will that none should perish (2 Peter 3:9; 1 Timothy 2:4-6; John 3:17; Romans 2:4-6,11). The only obstacle in the accomplishment of God's plan is a person's will. God did not create us to be like robots under His control; no, He gave us a free will – the will to accept His offer of salvation, or to reject it. But as the writer to the Hebrews expresses:

> *How shall we escape if we neglect so great a salvation, which at the first began to be spoken by the Lord, and was confirmed to us by those who heard Him* (Hebrews 2:3).

God takes the initiative by calling everyone to repentance, and this is the first step towards salvation.

How does God call people to repentance?

- by **His Word** (Romans 10:16,17; 2 Thessalonians 2:14,15)
- by **His Spirit** who convicts a person of sin (John 16:8; Hebrews 3:7,8)
- by **providence**; the result of His goodness, and sometimes His judgements (Romans 2:4; Isaiah 26:9; Psalm 107:6)
- through **His servants** who preach the Gospel, as the Lord commanded believers to do (Romans 10:14,15).

God is willing and able to help people take this first step. His Spirit causes a conviction of sin to well up within the hearts of people. The weight and guilt of sin brings about repentance which is a true sorrow for sin, accompanied by a sincere effort to not sin (Acts 2:37-39). In Scripture, we read, "*If we confess our sins, He is faithful and just to forgive us our sins and to cleanse us from all unrighteousness*" (1 John 1:9). Jesus preached, "*Repent, and believe in the gospel*" (Mark 1:15).

Belief is the second necessary step to salvation. With belief comes faith in Jesus Christ. Scripture teaches that we are saved by faith. *"For by grace you have been saved through faith, and that not of yourselves; it is the gift of God"* (Ephesians 2:8; Titus 3:4-6; Acts 16:31; Romans 5:1; 10:9,10). Faith, then, is a gift of God that comes to us through His Word and by looking to Jesus Christ (Romans 10:17; Hebrews 12:2). Can you understand how important it is for people to read and hear the Word of God? That is why it is necessary for Bibles to be given to all, and for ministries like *100 Huntley Street* and the program I host in the Arabic language, *Light For All Nations*, to be on the airwaves.

The Experience of Salvation

When a person has faith in Jesus Christ, in that instant he or she experiences salvation! It is an intellectual, spiritual, and emotional experience. It is a revelation of knowing that now you are saved and, if you should die, you are sure to have eternal life with God. The emotions may vary from a quiet peace to an explosion of joy or even tears of joy, but always with an emotion of gratitude to God.

What is involved in salvation?

What happens in that instant moment of salvation? Although the points are numbered, this does not mean they are in chronological order, for these things happen simultaneously.

1. **Conversion** is turning to God and away from sin. God pardons the person's sin and gives him or her a new heart.

2. **Justification** is when the saved person receives a new legal standing before God. It is a standing of favour and no longer one of condemnation, since the penalty of sin has been removed through Jesus Christ's gra-

cious sacrifice of Himself upon the cross, and because God imputes the righteousness of Christ to the believer (2 Corinthians 5:21).

3. **Regeneration** is the production of a new creature. The saved person now has a new nature (2 Corinthians 5:17; 2 Peter 1:4). He or she has experienced a new birth or has been born again to become a child of God, and is now able to have fellowship and communion with Him (John 3:3). This new birth is conditioned on faith in the crucified and resurrected Lord Jesus Christ (1 Peter 1:3,4), and is accomplished through the work of the Holy Spirit (Titus 3:5).

4. **Adoption** is involved in salvation. The saved person has a new position of honour before God, and he or she has a new and vital union with Jesus Christ who provides this assurance:

   I will not leave you orphans; I will come to you. A little while longer and the world will see Me no more, but you will see Me. Because I live, you will live also. At that day you will know that I am in My Father, and you in Me, and I in you (John 14:18-20).

   The Apostle Paul especially taught about adoption as one of the benefits of salvation (Galatians 4:4-7; Romans 8:15-17; Ephesians 1:5).

5. **Sanctification** occurs at the time of salvation, but is also an ongoing process in the life of the believer (1 Peter 1:14-16). It is the process of conforming to the image of Jesus Christ (Romans 8:29,30), being separated or consecrated unto God, and being made pure and holy. With sanctification comes the fruit of the Spirit, the strength to

overcome temptation, and the ability to live a life pleasing to God and in fellowship with Him. Sanctification of the believer is possible because of the blood that Jesus Christ shed on Calvary. In Scripture, we read,

> *But if we walk in the light as He is in the light, we have fellowship with one another, and the blood of Jesus Christ His Son cleanses us from all sin* (1 John 1:7; 1 Thessalonians 5:23).

There are many blessings and wonderful results of salvation. With our sins forgiven (having been redeemed by the Lamb, our Lord Jesus), we are reconciled to God and become the children of God (John 1:12; Ephesians 1:7). We become saints, a new creation, and partakers of His divine nature (2 Corinthians 5:17; 2 Peter 1:4), with our names written in the Lamb's Book of Life. The most wonderful experience of salvation will be when we see Jesus face to face and live with Him forever.

Have you experienced this wonderful work of God's grace through Jesus Christ? I urge you today to repent and believe in the Lord Jesus and you will be saved to enjoy the blessings of true fellowship with God.

Chapter 24

The Supremacy of Jesus Christ

The Lord Jesus Christ stands supreme over anyone else who ever lived or ever will live, for there is no one greater than Him. He is superior in every respect. His teachings, His miracles, and His holy and pure life display His supremacy. The Psalmist poetically expressed of the Great King: "*You are fairer than the sons of men; grace is poured upon Your lips; therefore God has blessed You forever*" (Psalm 45:2).

How is Jesus Superior?

1. **He came from above.** Jesus had no beginning and He has no end. He is the Alpha and Omega (Revelation 1:8,11). He is the eternal Son of God who came from heaven. He will reign forever upon His heavenly throne (Hebrews 1:8). John the Baptist did not hesitate to confess that Jesus was greater than he was, saying, "*He who comes from above is above all*" (John 3:31; 1:27).

2. **He is the Creator of all things.** He was present before the foundation of the world was laid. In fact, He laid the foundation. He was the Master Planner. All things were created by Him and for Him (Colossians 1:16) – for His pleasure, for His purposes, and for His glory. Nothing created could ever be greater than the One who created.

3. **His position.** He is the Son of God, the God-Man. With the incarnation, Jesus became a perfect Man, yet remained wholly God. No other person can come close to any comparison with Jesus, for He has all the attributes of God. Jesus is divine in every way – His nature is divine, His love is divine, and His light is divine. Jesus is:

   ...the image of the invisible God, the firstborn over all creation.... And He is before all things, and in Him all things consist. And He is the head of the body, the church, who is the beginning, the firstborn from the dead, that in all things He may have the pre-eminence (Colossians 1:15,17,18).

4. **His work.** He alone could provide salvation for the world. He offered Himself as the sinless and perfect sacrifice once and for all (Hebrews 9:14,15). Only Jesus could satisfy the justice of God and please Him. Because of His atoning work, Jesus has the power and authority to forgive sins, and fulfill His promise of granting eternal life to those who believe in Him. Jesus ushered in a new and better covenant, being a heavenly Priest or Mediator whose work is superior to that of Aaron and the Old Covenant's Levitical system (Hebrews 7). We read in Hebrews 8:6:

But now He has obtained a more excellent ministry, inasmuch as He is also Mediator of a better covenant, which was established on better promises.

Examples of Jesus' Superiority

The whole epistle to the Hebrews is devoted to showing the superiority of Jesus in all respects. To express this superiority, the writer repeatedly used words such as "better," "more perfect," "new," "more excellent," and "heavenly." Jesus is superior to the angels, for they worship Him (Hebrews 1:4). He is superior to all the great men of the Bible. He is superior to Adam, for through Adam came sin and death, but through Jesus came salvation and eternal life (Romans 5:9-21; John 5:21,26; 1 Corinthians 15:22). Jesus is referred to as the *"last Adam"* and the *"heavenly Man"* (1 Corinthians 15:45-49), for He is the firstborn of a new creation and He imparts a new nature (Colossians 1:15; 2 Corinthians 5:17).

Jesus is superior to Abraham, for Abraham paid tithes to Melchizedek who symbolized the heavenly eternal High Priest, our Lord Jesus (Hebrews 7:1-10). Even Jesus Himself expressed His superiority over Abraham by saying, *"Your father Abraham rejoiced to see My day, and he saw it and was glad"* (John 8:56). When questioned about Abraham having seen Him, Jesus responded, *"Most assuredly, I say to you, before Abraham was, I AM"* (John 8:58). Jesus is superior because He is pre-existent. He is the Great I AM.

Jesus is superior to Moses. The writer to the Hebrews spoke of Jesus, saying,

For this One has been counted worthy of more glory than Moses, inasmuch as He who built the house has more honour than the house (Hebrews 3:3).

Not only is Jesus greater than Moses, but He is greater than any of the other prophets (Hebrews 1:1-3). True prophets spoke the word of God, but Jesus *is* the Word of God. The Apostle John called Him the *Logos* (Greek for *word*, John 1:1) which implies that Jesus has the very thoughts, words, and personhood of God, since He is God. In fact, Jesus is the One who sent the prophets (Matthew 23:34). They testified of Him (John 5:39; Acts 10:42,43). He gave them the words to say, and imparted His wisdom to them, just as He continues to do today for those who serve Him (Luke 21:15). No other prophet or spiritual leader spoke as Jesus spoke, for as Jesus said, *"The words that I speak to you are spirit, and they are life"* (John 6:63).

Jesus is superior to Joshua who brought the children of Israel into a place of temporal rest; but the rest that Jesus gives is complete and eternal (Hebrews 4:8-11).

Jonah was considered a great prophet of God who changed the course of history, but Jesus said, concerning Himself: *"A greater [Prophet] than Jonah is here"* (Luke 11:32). Likewise, Jesus said He was greater than Solomon, the wisest man who ever lived (Luke 11:31). In the book of Proverbs, wisdom is often personified (Proverbs 8), and in many instances it foreshadows Jesus, who is *"wisdom from God"* (1 Corinthians 1:30). This divine wisdom became incarnate with Jesus Christ *"in whom are hidden all the treasures of wisdom and knowledge"* (Colossians 2:3).

King David is yet another great person of the Old Testament with whom Jesus is compared and found to be superior. Although Jesus is called by the Messianic name *Son of David*, He is more than just that. He is the Lord over David. He is greatly exalted and sits upon the heavenly throne (Acts 2:33-36; Luke 20:41-44). David had prophesied concerning Jesus: *"For You will not leave my soul in Sheol, nor will You allow Your Holy One to see corruption"* (Psalm 16:10). Jesus arose from the dead and is alive and reigning forever, but David died and his body saw decay (Acts 2:25-29; 13:35-37). Not only is Jesus superior to the great spiritual men of the Bible, He is also superior to the spiritual institutions, such as the temple or the Sabbath. Jesus said: *"But I say to you that in this place there is One greater than the temple,"* and He continued in the same context to say of Himself, *"For the Son of Man is Lord even of the Sabbath"* (Matthew 12:6,8).

Jesus' Rightful Place of Honour

The Apostle Paul clearly understood the supremacy of Jesus. In His letter to the believers of Colosse, he showed in numerous ways the superiority or pre-eminence of Jesus, who is the believer's all-sufficient Saviour (Colossians 1:28; 2:3,10; 3:1-4). Paul wrote to warn the church of false teachings that would degrade Jesus. One must have a proper understanding and belief in who Jesus is in order to keep the pure faith and combat heresy. In Jesus *"dwells all the fullness of the Godhead bodily...the head of all principality and power"* (Colossians 2:9,10). Jesus is Lord of all! He is the head of the church (Colossians 1:18), and as such, Christians must be submissive and obedient to Him. Jesus is the believer's hope of glory (Colossians 1:27; Hebrews 2:10). God has highly exalted Him above everyone and everything, and...

> *...given Him the name which is above every name, that at the name of Jesus every knee should bow...and...every tongue should confess that Jesus Christ is Lord, to the glory of God the Father* (Philippians 2:9-11).

In the book of Revelation, our Lord Jesus is revealed in His glory as the King of kings and Lord of lords (Revelation 19:16) who reigns supreme and judges the world.

Isn't He worthy of your allegiance? Believe in Jesus and submit to Him. You will experience His salvation, deliverance, rest, and marvellous love – a divine love that the world cannot offer or comprehend. Jesus is supreme in His love, which is unconditional and sacrificial. He died on the cross for you because He loves you and wants to save you from sin and death. Call upon His glorious name and you will be saved (Acts 16:31). Enthrone Jesus upon your heart for that is His rightful place of honour.

Chapter 25

The Uniqueness of Christianity

CHRISTIANITY is not merely a religion, which is a system of beliefs. It is more. Biblical Christianity is a relationship with the Lord Jesus Christ, and this makes it unique. Our faith is not only based on His teachings, but more importantly, it is based on His personhood – who He is. Therefore, a correct understanding and belief of Jesus is necessary for true Christianity. It is not based on subjective notions, but rather objective facts.

Why is Christianity unique?

1. **It revolves around a living person**, the risen Lord Jesus Christ, and is founded upon who He is and what He accomplished, namely our redemption from sin (1 Peter 1:18-21). Other religions revolve around their founder's teachings, rules, regulations, and rituals. Jesus communicates and interacts with His people even today. His presence is among us. He listens to us and answers our

prayers. He has the power to heal, transform lives, and save. For the believer, Jesus is everything (Acts 17:28).

2. **It is based upon historical facts and the revelation of God in the Bible.** Archaeological discoveries have never disproved anything spoken of in the Bible; rather, time and time again, they have confirmed its truth. Eyewitnesses confirmed that Jesus was who He claimed to be, and we believe because of our conviction of the truth. Many people have tried to prove that the Bible is false, but their attempts have failed. There is, however, overwhelming evidence that the Bible is true, such as the evidence from prophecies. There are over 2,000 prophecies in the Bible. Many of them have already been accurately fulfilled, which attest to the divine origin of the Bible.

3. **The relationship it affords with Jesus offers a promise of salvation and eternal life** in heaven with the Lord. We are not left in doubt as to whether or not we will merit God's favour and live in heaven. No, we are made certain of it because of God's Word. We know without a doubt that Jesus is our Saviour. His death, resurrection, and ascension gave credibility to the truth of His message and the truth of His claims. Christianity is the only religion that offers the assurance and security of salvation in the present, and from the time we first believed until we breathe our last breath and beyond. We have the assurance:

   - of a new life (1 John 3:14)
   - of divine care (Romans 8:28)
   - that God hears our prayers (1 John 5:13)

- of a happy ending (2 Corinthians 5:1,5-8).

All this brings wonderful peace and hope to the believer. We know that one day we will be with Jesus in heaven.

4. **It is the only religion that teaches salvation is a free gift of God's grace.** There is nothing a person can do to merit salvation, since it is received through faith, apart from works. The greatest teacher of Christianity, other than Jesus, was the Apostle Paul, who explained: "*A man is justified by faith apart from the deeds of the law*" (Romans 3:28). Every other religion is works-oriented in an attempt to please and appease its deity. This does not mean that Christianity has a lower standard of works or good deeds than other religions. On the contrary. Our faith leads us to do good works (Ephesians 2:8-10; James 2:17), and the standards of Christianity are so high that the natural man could never attain it. Take for example the great Sermon on the Mount. Clearly Jesus taught that the standard for humankind is perfection. He said, "*You shall be perfect, just as your Father in heaven is perfect*" (Matthew 5:48). On our own this is impossible, for every person is a sinner (Romans 3:23). This is why Jesus died, shed His precious blood and became our Redeemer, that through Him, we might have His righteousness. No amount of good deeds or sincerity will ever gain a person the right to go to heaven. We have no right, except through Jesus who washes away our sin (Titus 3:5). When we have faith in Jesus, the only perfect Man, we become justified in God's sight (Romans 3:25,26).

5. **It is clearly of divine origin,** for it goes against the very nature of humankind. A nature that is full of pride, like

that of the "self-made man," who prides himself in attaining his goals without help from anyone. Christianity confesses that we need a Saviour, and without Him, we are lost (Ephesians 2:4,5).

6. **It also has a high and humanly impossible, unattainable standard of righteousness.** What human being would invent a standard of righteousness they could never hope to achieve? In fact, other religions that have been founded by mere, sinful men consist of rules and regulations that can be achieved through the human effort of the devout and pious. This attests to their human origin. Only God would give us a standard only He could attain. Jesus, the God-Man, was the only person to ever attain it. Since He was perfect and full of grace, He can purchase our salvation and give it to us as a wonderful, gracious, and undeserved gift. Other religions were started because of man's attempt to search for the supernatural and truth, appease his innate sense of sin and guilt, and find favour with his god. But Christianity is the account of God's search for humankind. *"For the Son of Man has come to seek and to save that which was lost"* (Luke 19:10; John 10:10). His love was the reason He has revealed Himself to us through His Son Jesus, and by His grace we are saved (Ephesians 2:8,9).

7. **It reveals God as the triune God** – God as the Father, God as the Son, and God as the Spirit (Matthew 28:19). Christianity reveals God as love (1 John 4:8,16) and as approachable, near, and personal (1 John 5:14,15; Ephesians 2:13,18; John 14:21). The triune God is revealed as being involved in the plan of redemption. We are loved and chosen by the Father, redeemed by the

Son, and our redemption is sealed by the Spirit (Ephesians 1:1-14).

8. **It is exclusive.** This does not mean that Christianity is only for some people and not for others. No, any person, from any ethnic background, has an open invitation to accept Jesus, believe in Him, and thereby become a Christian (1 Timothy 2:3-6). The exclusiveness of Christianity is found in its claims, which in today's pluralistic society is not politically correct. As Christians, however, we are called to present the Gospel of truth, and not compromise, even if it offends people. We are warned to not take away or alter the truth of its message, for Scripture tells us that the person who does this is accursed (Galatians 1:9). In fact, a true presentation of the Gospel should offend people and this is to be expected. Both Jesus and the Apostle Paul said that the Gospel would be a stumbling block and will offend many, resulting in the persecution of the believer (1 Peter 2:7,8; 1 Corinthians 1:23; Matthew 5:11; 11:6; John 6:60-66). Jesus said to unbelievers, *"The world cannot hate you, but it hates Me because I testify of it that its works are evil"* (John 7:7). Jesus exposed the evil in the world, and this offended many people who were content to live as they pleased and not as God pleased. The truth is often difficult to bear, but when we believe the truth of the Gospel, it is the truth that sets us free (John 8:32). When we do not know the truth, then we are in bondage.

There is no such thing as subjective truth. What is true for one person is true for all. Truth is truth. We know that truth exists in the world and that it can only be discovered.

A certain belief will not necessarily be true just because we think it is true, or feel it to be true. No, truth is always objective. Two opposing viewpoints cannot both be right. With this in mind, being politically correct is impossible. Therefore, I will proceed (and may offend some people), for I have been called to preach the truth.

How is Christianity exclusive?

1. **The God of Christianity** is claimed to be the only true God (Jeremiah 10:10; Jude 25).

2. **The Bible** is claimed to be the Word of God and the only true revelation from God (Isaiah 8:20; Revelation 22:18,19; 2 Timothy 3:16).

3. **The Biblical way to salvation** is the only way to be eternally saved. There is no other way (John 3:36). No matter how good, religious or sincere a person may be, unless he or she has faith in Jesus, they will not be saved:

   Nor is there salvation in any other, for there is no other name under heaven given among men by which we must be saved (Acts 4:12).

4. **Jesus Christ** claims to be the only way to God, the only way of salvation, and the only way to eternal life in heaven (John 3:16,17). Jesus said, *"I am the Way, the Truth, and the Life. No one comes to the Father except through Me"* (John 14:6).

These claims are either totally true or totally false. Now, some may argue that Biblical Christianity is narrow-minded, but even though it may be narrow, it is still true. Jesus taught that the way to life is narrow. It is not always an easy way, but it is the right and only way to salvation (Matthew 7:13,14). The teachings of Jesus are either totally true or totally false. It is absurd to believe some of the claims of Jesus and to reject others. You must either accept them or totally reject them; accept Jesus or reject Him. If He was who He claimed to be, then we must give Him our allegiance. If His claims were untrue, then He could only be considered a madman. The study of the evidence, however, strongly supports the truth of Jesus' claims. He is the only way to salvation and those who do not believe in Him will be lost for eternity (1 John 2:22,23).

Again, in today's world, even to say such a thing is politically incorrect, but that does not make it untrue. For the sake of the lost and for those who have yet to hear the Gospel, Bible-believing Christians must have a zeal to evangelize all people. May God help us in this great task; a task that, because of His great love, He commanded us to do. If you do not know Jesus personally, and have not yet experienced His salvation, I pray you will believe in Him today. As Jesus said to the sinful woman, *"Your faith has saved you. Go in peace"* (Luke 7:50). In the Arabic language, when we say good-bye, we always say, *"Ma Salami"* meaning *"Go in peace."* But this can only be true when a person knows our unique Saviour Jesus Christ.

Chapter 26

THE UNIQUE CHRIST

ACCORDING to the dictionary, the word "*unique*" means "*being the only one of a particular type; without equal or like*" (Collins Pocket Reference English Dictionary, Canadian Edition, Harper Collins Publishers Ltd. Toronto: 1998). Certainly in our study thus far of the many aspects of Jesus' life and work, we have seen how He is indeed unequalled. There was never another like Him, nor will there ever be. He is the one and only Son of God, who was sent from heaven to be born as a baby on earth. This significant birthday is the reason for our Christmas celebration! We have much to celebrate. If only all the people who put up lights and Christmas trees understood the real meaning of Christmas, and knew the unique Person whose birthday they were celebrating. Jesus came that we might have salvation and know Him in a personal way – to have a close relationship with Him.

Jesus is not just another great teacher, moralist or religious founder among many others in history. No, Jesus stands alone and supreme. Let us consider the four main factors that make the Lord Jesus unique.

How is Jesus Christ unique?

1. **He fulfilled numerous prophecies** in detail concerning His coming, purpose, death, resurrection, and many other things spoken of Him hundreds of years before He came. There are specific prophecies given by different people – from a king to a shepherd – in different circumstances and at different times. Yet they are harmonious, not contradictory, accidental or speculative. The probability of so many prophecies being fulfilled in one person is impossible in the natural sense. With Jesus, however, it was clearly supernatural, for God had a divine plan and was working in history according to His purpose.

2. **His miraculous conception and virgin birth**. Adam, the first man, was created by God, but every other person, except Jesus, has been born biologically of a man and a woman. Not so with Jesus. No, He was born of a woman only through a miracle of God (Genesis 3:15; Isaiah 7:14; Galatians 4:4), for nothing is impossible for Him.

3. **His sinless life.** No one else but Jesus could truthfully claim to have never sinned in the course of His life. He lived a pure and holy life pleasing to God:

   And He who sent Me is with Me. The Father has not left Me alone, for I always do those things that please Him (John 8:29).

   For the rest of humanity, the wrath of God is upon us because of our sin, unless we have been redeemed by the blood of Jesus. Jesus, the pure, holy, unblemished Lamb of God whose blood washes away sin (John 1:29; John 3:36). No one could truthfully accuse Jesus of sin, since in Him was no sin (John 8:46; Hebrews 1:9; 4:15; 7:26; 2 Corinthians 5:21). His friends confessed that He was sinless (1 Peter 2:22; 1 John 3:5). So did His enemies, such as Pontius Pilate who said, *"I find no fault in Him at all"* (John 18:38); and Judas, His betrayer, who confessed, *"I have sinned by betraying innocent blood"* (Matthew 27:4). Jesus did nothing shameful, embarrassing, or wrong. He was the only Person who did not need to ask for forgiveness, yet He taught us about confession and forgiveness. He is the example of perfection and goodness. Although born of the Virgin Mary, He came into the world untainted by the original sin or the sinful nature from Adam. He is the world's moral miracle, innocent from His birth and innocent He remains. Because of the miracle of the incarnation, Jesus was the embodiment of truth, perfection, light, and holiness. He is the absolute and ultimate perfection – the beauty of perfection and the example of perfection. He is the Holy One, the Righteous Son of God, who is worthy to be praised and adored throughout all generations and forevermore.

4. **He is the God-Man**, having deity and perfect humanity in perfect union. As such, He was qualified to be the Redeemer and Saviour of the world. The angel announced to Joseph on that first Christmas that *"Immanuel...God with us,"* would be the Saviour of the world (Matthew 1:23). Not only would Jesus bring salvation to the world, but He is the Creator of the world:

All things were created through Him and for Him. And He is before all things, and in Him all things consist (Colossians 1:16b-17).

In many ways, both directly and indirectly, Jesus claimed to be God. What other man could have done so and been believed by so many?

Jesus was both fully God and fully Man. This is the great mystery of the incarnation. God humbled Himself. He became a little Baby, born to a poor family, for a great purpose. His incarnation was the solution for humankind. Since God is just and holy, He hates sin. And because God is love and mercy, He loves the sinner. This is where the love of God is manifested, by sending His Son Jesus into the world. The justice of God is met through the redemptive work of Jesus Christ upon the cross. Only a perfect Human could qualify to be the Redeemer, and Jesus was just that. He solved the sin problem of the world by being the Great Substitute who died in our place. By His death, He paid the price of sin for the whole world. Only Jesus could meet all these demands (Isaiah 53:6; 1 John 2:2), thus He is the only Mediator who can reconcile us with God.

The uniqueness of Christ continues...

5. **His dealings with people.** No one in His day and age treated people as He did. He treated everyone equally since He loves everyone the same. He stopped a large crowd of people in order to heal a blind beggar and give him spiritual sight (Luke 18:35-43). He took the time to deal with the despised and unwanted tax collector and bring salvation to him and his household (Luke 19:1-10).

He did not condemn the woman caught in adultery, but demanded that she sin no more (John 8:1-11). He dealt with the enemies of His people in a loving and kind way. He offered "Living Water" to the Samaritans (John 4:9-15,39; Luke 9:56). He taught about forgiveness and loving one's enemies, and He demonstrated it by forgiving those who crucified Him (Luke 23:34; Matthew 5:44). He showed love, compassion, and forgiveness to Peter who denied Him. He cared for everyone. He healed. He fed the hungry. He never rejected anyone. He was truly our perfect example. The proper response to Him is to bow in reverence, awe, and adoration.

6. **His teachings are unique and unparalleled.** They cannot be compared to the teachings of anyone else who has ever lived, since Jesus spoke with divine authority, wisdom, and power. His words are words of life and truth, and no other teachings can compare with the results of the teachings of Jesus. Certainly, He alone has had the most influence throughout history until today.

7. **His relationship with God, the Father, and His great miracles.** He restored blinded eyes and raised the dead to life. By His own power, Jesus raised Himself to life again after He had been crucified and in the grave for three days. Only Jesus arose from the dead and is *"alive forevermore"* (Revelation 1:18). He had told His disciples that He was going to die, saying:

   Therefore My Father loves Me, because I lay down My life that I may take it again. No one takes it from Me, but I lay it down of Myself. I have power to lay it down, and I have power to take it again (John 10:17,18).

8. **He was the only person who was born for the express purpose of dying.** Jesus came to lay down His life. Now, please don't let this put a damper on your next Christmas celebration. For Jesus' birth is made more joyous because it shows us the great love of God, who gave up His one and only Son. That Son then left God's side on the throne in heaven and came to a lowly people, in a lowly land, to be our Saviour!

9. **The uniqueness of His death itself.** Now, we know that all people, in a body of flesh and blood, will die. Jesus had a normal human body as well. So how is His death unique? Jesus said that it was of His own power that He laid down His life. It was not the Romans who ultimately killed Him. No mere man could take His life, for He is *the Life*, but it was of His own will that He died. We read in Scripture that upon the cross, *"He said, 'It is finished!' And bowing His head, He gave up His spirit"* (John 19:30). By His own will, Jesus dismissed His spirit from His body. No other person could have the power to do this. Even the soldiers were surprised at how quickly Jesus died upon the cross.

10. **He died vicariously, or in our place,** as the sacrificial Lamb. He redeemed us from our sin and the penalty of death, and gave us eternal life with Him. He earned the right to be our Redeemer (Philippians 2:5-11). There has never been another person on earth so full of love and compassion as Jesus, our Lord and our God.

He loves you today. He was born in Bethlehem about 2,000 years ago because of His great love for you. You can have forgiveness of sins and real life by coming to Him and believing in Him. The Lord Jesus Christ, the most unique

Person of all ages, has extended to you this invitation: *"Come to Me, all you who labour and are heavy laden, and I will give you rest"* (Matthew 11:28). Who, but Jesus, could make such a promise? For the believer, He gives rest, hope, strength, encouragement, and peace to the soul (Matthew 12:21; John 14:27; Luke 10:19; 24:49). Who, but Jesus, could promise and deliver the security of salvation and an everlasting life with Him? All praise and glory to our wonderful Lord Jesus!

Special Note

If you would like a *100 Huntley Street* prayer partner to pray with you for salvation, please call the prayer line nearest you. The phone numbers are listed on page 217 for your convenience. It's the most important decision you can make – one with eternal value!

Light For All Nations Ministries

"Reaching the unreached with the Gospel Message"

Nizar Shaheen is the president and host of Light For All Nations Ministries, an effective and vital evangelistic television outreach in the Arabic language. The weekly television program, ***Light For All Nations***, is seen in Canada, some parts of the United States and Europe, in the Middle East, and in North Africa with a potential audience of over 400 million people. The Lord is greatly using this ministry to spread the Gospel, and many people have come to know the salvation of Jesus Christ through its witness.

Light For All Nations is a non-profit, charitable organization that is supported solely by the giving of missions-minded people.

For information contact:
Light For All Nations,
P.O. Box 85300, Burlington, Ontario, Canada, L7R 4K3

E-mail: lfan@lfan.com   Web site: www.lfan.com
Telephone: 905-335-0700

The Crossroads Ministry Story

It All Began In 1962...

In Pembroke, located in the Ottawa Valley of northeastern Ontario, David Mainse was the pastor of an area church. It was there, in 1962, David and his wife Norma-Jean first broadcast the Gospel on black and white TV sets. The program was called ***Crossroads***.

As the Mainse family moved to other centres to pastor, the television ministry moved with them. It grew in popularity and was aired on more and more stations.

In 1977, the ministry of Crossroads launched daily programming across Canada from God-given facilities in downtown Toronto at an address after which the telecast was named: ***100 Huntley Street.***

Crossroads' Mission Statement

"The key objective of Crossroads Christian Communications Incorporated is to add to and bring unity to the body of Christ through direct and indirect evangelism; to enhance and augment the ministry of the local church; and to build understanding, credibility and attractiveness of life in Jesus Christ.

"This will be accomplished by the creative use of television and other media, together with other activities which respond to the mission conscience and needs of the constituency. The responsibility for outreach is to the world. Outside North America, C.C.C.I. responds only to the requests from organized and established Christian leadership. The role is as a catalyst to the development of indigenous and self-supporting ministry."

Accountability

Crossroads Christian Communications Inc. is federally chartered in both Canada and the United States as a charitable, non-profit organization. As such, it is funded wholly through free-will offerings. Crossroads is audited annually by Price Waterhouse Lybrand. Financial statements are available upon written request.

Crossroads receives the annual Seal of Financial Accountability from the Canadian Council of Christian Charities.

David & Norma-Jean

Ron & Ann

Reynold & Kathy

100 Huntley Street

Cal

Norm

Lorna

Rhonda

Nizar

The Crossroads Ministry

is made possible through the generous gifts of people like you who believe in Life-Changing Television. As many as 1.5 million individuals tune in to the ***100 Huntley Street*** broadcast every week.

24-Hour Prayer Ministry

Prayer lines are available 24 hours a day – a lifeline for many in crisis.

Crossroads receives calls from over 30,000 needy people each month. Over 200 volunteer prayer partners donate 30,000 hours each year to minister and pray for such needs as salvation, healing, substance abuse, suicide, emotional problems and family concerns.

Crossroads also provides helpful ministry materials on many relevant subjects like anger, depression, grief, healing, reconciliation, etc.

To help new Christians become firmly established in their relationship with God, Crossroads uses in-depth Bible study courses. New Christians are also encouraged to join a local church for further spiritual growth and fellowship with other believers.

Crossroads Prayer Lines

A Crossroads prayer partner would love to pray with you for any special need you may be facing today. Simply call our prayer line nearest you:

Vancouver, BC	**604-430-1212**
Calgary, AB	**403-284-4721**
Edmonton, AB	**780-944-0742**
Regina, SK	**306-781-8970**
Winnipeg, MB	**204-949-9414**
Burlington, ON or USA	**905-335-0100**
Toronto, ON	**416-929-1500**
Montreal, QC	**514-935-8814**
Quebec City, QC	**418-864-7448**
Saint John, NB	**506-674-2400**
Halifax, NS	**902-455-2600**
St. John's, NF	**709-738-2731**

Hearing impaired TDD 905-335-6104

A Special Invitation: If you live in the Toronto/Burlington area and would like to join the ministry as a prayer partner, call the National Ministry Centre at:

905-332-6400, ext. 2383

Crossroads' Conway School of Broadcasting and Communications

Twice each year, Crossroads conducts a unique, 16-week course. This fully-accredited course in Christian television production is designed especially to prepare those with a vision to start Christian programming in their own countries. Crossroads has trained over 1,350 students from 72 countries thus far.

Crossroads' Emergency Response and Development Fund

This is a fund established out of compassion for people in areas of the world hit by disasters such as earthquakes, famine and war. Crossroads has sent millions of dollars in relief to the world's needy.

The Walk of Faith

The Walk of Faith is a lovely walkway around the Crossroads Centre. Along the walkway are engraved granite stones which have been donated in honour or in memory of special people. Find out how you can join the Walk of Faith by calling: **1-800-265-3100**

Other Crossroads TV Outreaches Sharing The Love of Jesus...

Rise & Shine
A morning breakfast show with news and inspiration.

Nite Lite
Middle-of-the-night open-line ministry.

T.Q.
Saturday morning children's programming with a positive message.

The NIRV
Teens reaching teens with music and discussion.